797,885 Books
are available to read at

Forgotten Books

www.ForgottenBooks.com

Forgotten Books' App
Available for mobile, tablet & eReader

ISBN 978-1-331-62830-9
PIBN 10214998

This book is a reproduction of an important historical work. Forgotten Books uses state-of-the-art technology to digitally reconstruct the work, preserving the original format whilst repairing imperfections present in the aged copy. In rare cases, an imperfection in the original, such as a blemish or missing page, may be replicated in our edition. We do, however, repair the vast majority of imperfections successfully; any imperfections that remain are intentionally left to preserve the state of such historical works.

Forgotten Books is a registered trademark of FB &c Ltd.
Copyright © 2015 FB &c Ltd.
FB &c Ltd, Dalton House, 60 Windsor Avenue, London, SW19 2RR.
Company number 08720141. Registered in England and Wales.

For support please visit www.forgottenbooks.com

1 MONTH OF FREE READING

at
www.ForgottenBooks.com

By purchasing this book you are eligible for one month membership to ForgottenBooks.com, giving you unlimited access to our entire collection of over 700,000 titles via our web site and mobile apps.

To claim your free month visit:
www.forgottenbooks.com/free214998

* Offer is valid for 45 days from date of purchase. Terms and conditions apply.

Similar Books Are Available from
www.forgottenbooks.com

Poems
by Edgar Allan Poe

The Complete Poetical Works and Letters of John Keats
by John Keats

Erotica
by Arthur Clark Kennedy

The Complete Poetical Works of John Milton
by John Milton

One Hundred Poems of Kabir
by Kabir

The Barons' Wars, Nymphidia, and Other Poems
by Michael Drayton

A Book of English Poetry
by George Beaumont

Poems: Sonnets, Lyrics, and Miscellaneous
by Edward Blackadder

The Book of Fairy Poetry
by Dora Owen

Chinese Poems
by Charles Budd

Coleridge's The Rime of the Ancient Mariner
And Other Poems, by Samuel Taylor Coleridge

Complaints; Containing Sundrie Small Poemes of the Worlds Vanitie
Whereof the Next Page Maketh Mention, by Edmund Spenser

The Complete Poetical Works of Geoffrey Chaucer
Now First Put Into Modern English, by John S. P. Tatlock

Cursor Mundi (The Cursor of the World)
A Northumbrian Poem of the XIVth Century, by Richard Morris

The Defence of the Bride Other Poems
by Anna Katharine Green

The Divine Comedy, Vol. 1
by Dante Alighieri

The Duke of Gandia
by Algernon Charles Swinburne

Eanthe
A Tale of the Druids, and Other Poems, by Sandford Earle

The Earthly Paradise
A Poem, by William Morris

The English Poems of George Herbert
Newly Arranged in Relation to His Life, by George Herbert Palmer

HISTORICAL EMBELLISHMENTS,

ILLUSTRATING THE POETICAL WORKS

OF

LORD BYRON.

Engraved from Original Paintings by
SIR THOMAS LAWRENCE, P.R.A.
H HOWARD, R.A.   A. E. CHALON, R.A.   T. STOTHARD, R.A.
R WESTALL, R.A. AND OTHER EMINENT ARTISTS.

A NEW AND ENLARGED EDITION, WITH DESCRIPTIVE LETTER-PRESS.

LONDON:
PUBLISHED BY SMITH, ELDER AND CO., CORNHILL.
1844.

PR
4377
B87
1844

1044503

PREFACE.

However popular and well known an author may be, it is seldom that his admirers are so conversant with the whole of his works, as to enable their memory to seize at once on the intention of the painter, who attempts to illustrate them, or to recal immediately the particular incident which he designs to embody, especially when such illustrations embrace a very large range of subjects.

To the young the poems of Lord Byron are often a forbidden treasure. To those, who are young no longer, and whose tastes were formed before the advent of that poet, the popular admiration has seemed to be an alarming heresy in literature; and, like the long blinded "Ursel" of Walter Scott, they have closed their eyes against the light which has streamed on all around them. From the minds of the busy a thousand whirling thoughts have swept away the images which were once impressed there; and, even in the breast of the thoughtful, it often happens, that nothing remains of the past intellectual banquet, but a vague and indistinct remembrance of the grief, and beauty and desolation described by the poet.

Of the numerous admirers of the "Byron Gallery," there has been, perhaps, scarcely one whose memory has not required a prompter to enable his understanding to partake of, and confirm the gratification of his pictorial taste; and this circumstance has induced the proprietors of the Work to append to each engraving some slight explanation of the subject illustrated: which, like a few notes of music—however rudely and unskilfully stricken—may recal the full and perfect, though half forgotten, melody, enjoyed in former years.

THE BYRON GALLERY.

LIST OF THE EMBELLISHMENTS.

TITLE.	PAINTER.	ENGRAVER.	REFERENCE.
AROLD	Sir T. Lawrence, P.R.A.	C. G. Lewis	Canto 4. Stanza 115*
	E. T. Parris	F. Bacon	Canto 1. Stanza 11
	W. Purser	E. Finden	Canto 2. Stanza 52
,	H. Richter	R. Staines	Canto 4. Stanza 177
UR	E. T. Parris	H. Cook	As rears her crest, &c.
ABYDOS	De Caisne	S. Sangster	Canto 1. Stanza 10
	H. Richter	W. Finden	Canto 1. Stanza 11
AIR	H. Richter	T. A. Dean	Canto 3. Stanza 3.
	H. Richter	R. Baker	Canto 3. Stanza 5
	S. J. E. Jones	W. Chevalier	Canto 2. Stanza 24
CORINTH	W. Penley	R. Staines	Stanza 19. Line 485
	E. C. Wood	W. Finden	Stanza 2
	H. Richter	W. Chevalier	Stanza 13
	J. P. Davis	J. Goodyear	Stanza 15
	H. Richter	H. T. Ryall	Stanza 23
	H. Richter	S. S. Smith	Stanza 89
	H. Richter	R. Staines	Stanza 6
ND	H. Richter	H. C. Shenton	Canto 4. Stanza 9
	H. Corbould	J. Romney	Act 1. Scene 1
	H. Howard, R.A.	F. Bacon	Act 2. Scene 2

* The Frontispiece.

LIST OF THE EMBELLISHMENTS.

TITLE.	PAINTER.	ENGRAVER.	REFERENCE.
Faliero	R. Westall, R.A.	W. Finden	Act 5. End of Scene 2
and Earth	H. Richter	E. J. Portbury	Part 1. Scene 3
apalus	E. T. Parris	G. A. Periam	Act 3. Scene 1
o Foscari	S. J. E. Jones	E. J. Portbury	Act 3. Last sentence
,,	T. Stothard, R.A.	E. J. Portbury	Act 5. Scene 1
ied Transformed	H. Richter	H. Cook	Part 1. Scene 1
of Idleness	H. Richter	W. Finden	Love's last Adieu
ltz	J. Stephanoff	S. S. Smith	Stanza 2
v Melodies	H. Richter	E. Finden	She walks in Beauty
,,	H. Richter	H. C. Shenton	Jephtha's Daughter
eam	H. Corbould	J. Goodyear	Stanza 2
f Athens	A. E. Chalon R.A.	H. T. Ryall	Occasional Poems — "Maid of Athens, ere we part"
ss Guiccioli	E. C. Wood	T. A. Dean	Occasional Poems — Stanzas to the Po.
	H. Richter	Charles Rolls	Canto 1. Stanza 92
	E. T. Parris	S. S. Smith	Canto 1. Stanza 97
	H. Richter	E. Finden	Canto 2. Stanza 185

Painted by E. T. Parris.　　　Engraved by F. Bacon.

HIS HOUSE, HIS HOME, HIS HERITAGE, HIS LANDS,
THE LAUGHING DAMES IN WHOM HE DID DELIGHT
WHOSE LARGE BLUE EYES, FAIR LOCKS, AND SNOWY HANDS,
MIGHT SHAKE THE SAINTSHIP OF AN ANCHORITE,
AND LONG HAD FED HIS YOUTHFUL APPETITE,
HIS GOBLETS BRIMM'D WITH EVERY COSTLY WINE,
AND ALL THAT MOTE TO LUXURY INVITE,
WITHOUT A SIGH HE LEFT,——

CHILDE HAROLD.

Published by Smith Elder & Cº Cornhill London.

CHILDE HAROLD.

Painted by Parris.]   [Engraved by Bacon.

CHILDE HAROLD, having exhausted all the pleasures of youth and early manhood, feels the fulness of satiety, loathing his fellow bacchanals, and the "laughing dames in whom he did delight."—

> "For he through sin's long labyrinth had run,
> Nor made atonement when he did amiss;
> Had sighed to many, though he loved but one,
> And that loved one, alas! could ne'er be his."

Some needless pains have been taken to exonerate Lord Byron from the imputation of debauchery here cast upon the Childe. His interior at Newstead, had, no doubt, been, in some points, loose and irregular enough; but it certainly never exhibited any thing of the profuse and sultanic luxury which the language in the text might seem to indicate. His household economy, while he remained at the abbey, is known to have been conducted on a very moderate scale; and, besides, his usual companions, though far from being averse to convivial indulgencies, were not only, as Mr. Moore says, "of habits and tastes too intellectual for mere vulgar debauchery, but assuredly, quite incapable of playing the parts of flatterers and parasites."

Nothing can be so absurd as to accumulate on an author every trait of character described in poetical portraiture. The spirit, and feelings, and opinions of the writer may be occasionally revealed, but to apply to Lord Byron's life at Newstead, the description of the voluptuous Childe, would be about as reasonable as to accuse Mrs. Siddons of poisoning and stabbing, because the attributes of tragedy form the back ground of her picture. In both the poem and the painting are revelations of the lofty bearing, the surpassing beauty, the peerless intellect which distinguished the gifted originals, and which must have had existence, ere they could have been rendered to the eye, and the understanding; but no further does the resemblance hold.

THE ALBANIAN.

PEERING DOWN EACH PRECIPICE, HIS GOAT
BROWSETH, AND, PENSIVE O'ER HIS SCATTER'D FLOCK
THE LITTLE SHEPHERD IN HIS WHITE CAPOTE
DOTH LEAN HIS BOYISH FORM ALONG THE ROCK.

CHILDE HAROLD.

Published by Smith, Elder & Co. Cornhill, London.

THE ALBANIAN.

Painted by Purser.] [Engraved by Finden.

"The Arnaout, or Albanese," says Lord Byron, "struck me forcibly by their resemblance to the Highlanders of Scotland, in dress, figure, and manner of living. Their very mountains seemed Caledonian, with a kinder climate. The kilt, though white: the spare active form: their dialect, Celtic in its sound, and their hardy habits, all carried me back to Morven. No nation are so detested and dreaded by their neighbours as the Albanese; the Greeks hardly regard them as Christians, nor the Turks as Moslems; and in fact, they are a mixture of both, and sometimes neither. Their habits are predatory—all are armed; and the red-shawled Arnaouts, the Montenegrins, Chimariots, and Gedges, are treacherous; the others differ somewhat in garb, and essentially in character: as far as my own experience goes, I can speak favourably. I was attended by two, an Infidel and a Mussulman, to Constantinople and every other part of Turkey that came within my observation; and more faithful in peril, or indefatigable in service are rarely to be found.

"The Albanians in general (I do not mean the cultivators of the earth in the provinces, who have also that appellation, but the mountaineers) have a fine cast of countenance. Their manner of walking is truly theatrical; but this strut is, probably, the effect of the capote, or long cloak depending from one their courage in desultory warfare is unquestionable."

> " Land of Albania! let me bend my eyes
> On thee, thou rugged nurse of savage men!
> The cross descends, thy minarets arise,
> And the pale crescent sparkles in the glen,
> Through many a cypress grove within each city's ken."

Drawn by H. Richter. Engraved by R. Staines.

OH! THAT THE DESERT WERE MY DWELLING-PLACE,
WITH ONE FAIR SPIRIT FOR MY MINISTER,
THAT I MIGHT ALL FORGET THE HUMAN RACE,
AND, HATING NO ONE, LOVE BUT ONLY HER!

CHILDE HAROLD.

CHILDE HAROLD.

Painted by Richter.] [Engraved by Staines.

The sadness that possessed the poet on finding that

" Life's enchanted cup but sparkled near the brim,"

even when he had filled again,

" And from a purer fount, on holier ground,
And deemed its spring perpetual : but in vain!"

the disappointed hope of finding a companion for his own giant mind in the dwarfish intellects that surrounded him : the fruitless search for sympathy and attachment in any human breast,—seem to have led to that beautiful and passionate burst of feeling, in which he describes his yearning for intercourse with the presiding spirit of the magnificent scenery which surrounded him.

"Oh! that the desert were my dwelling place,
With one fair spirit for my minister,
That I might all forget the human race
And, hating no one, love but only her!
Ye elements!—in whose ennobling stir
I feel myself exalted—can ye not
Accord me such a being? Do I err
In deeming such inhabit many a spot?
Though with them to converse can rarely be our lot."*

---

* Those acquainted with Lord Byron's poetry will remember how finely this idea is enlarged upon in the fourth Canto of Childe Harold, in the stanzas referring to Numa and Egeria.

CHILDE HAROLD.

That this sadness was not imaginary, is evident from the following extract from the journal of his Swiss tour:—" I am disposed to be pleased. I am a lover of nature, and an admirer of beauty. I can bear fatigue, and welcome privation, and have seen some of the noblest views in the world. But in all this,—the recollection of bitterness, and, more especially, of recent and more home desolation, which must accompany me through life, has preyed upon me here; and neither the music of the shepherd, the crashing of the avalanche, nor the torrent, the mountain, the glacier, the forest, nor the cloud, have for one moment lightened the weight upon my heart, nor enabled me to lose my own wretched identity, in the majesty, and the power, and the glory, around, above and beneath me."

LEILA.

AS REARS HER CREST THE RUFFLED SWAN,
  AND SPURNS THE WAVE WITH WINGS OF PRIDE
WHEN PASS THE STEPS OF STRANGER MAN
  ALONG THE BANKS THAT BOUND HER TIDE,
THUS ROSE FAIR LEILA'S WHITER NECK——
THUS ARM'D WITH BEAUTY WOULD SHE CHECK
INTRUSIONS GLANCE.——

THE GIAOUR.

LEILA.

Painted by E. T. Parris.] [Engraved by H. Cook.

It seems impertinent to offer any observation on a tale so well known, and so universally admired as the " Giaour ;" we shall, therefore, content ourselves by recalling briefly to the reader's recollection, that Leila, the beautiful slave of the Turkish Hassan, loved, and was beloved by a young "Infidel;" and, on the discovery of her guilt, suffered the secret penalty of such an offence in the East, being tied up in a sack and flung into the sea. Her lover deeply avenged her death by the slaughter of her relentless master, and then concludes in a convent a life wasted in bitter regrets for the loss of Leila, and soothed only by the remembrance of gratified vengeance.

The summary justice inflicted by Moslem husbands, is playfully vindicated by Lord Byron in one of his gayer poems.

> " If now and then there happen'd a slight slip,
> Little was heard of criminal or crime ;
> The story scarcely pass'd a single lip,
> The sack and sea had settled all in time.
>   *   *
> No scandals made the daily press a curse,
> Morals were better, and the fish no worse."

From the set of "orient pearls at random strung," of which the Giaour is composed, we select the following description of Leila's loveliness :—

LEILA.

Her eye's dark charm 'twere vain to tell
But gaze on that of the Gazelle,
It will assist thy fancy well;
As large, as languishingly dark,
But Soul beam'd forth in every spark
That darted from beneath the lid
Bright as the jewel of Giamschid.*
* * * *
The cygnet nobly walks the water;
So moved on earth Circassia's daughter,
The loveliest bird of Franguestan! †
As rears her crest the ruffled swan,
   And spurns the wave with wings of pride,
When pass the steps of stranger man,
   Along the banks that bound her tide;
Thus rose fair Leila's whiter neck,—
Thus armed with beauty would she check
Intrusion's glance, till Folly's gaze
Shrunk from the charms it meant to praise."

* The celebrated fabulous ruby of Sultan Giamschid, the embellisher of Istakhar; from its splendour named Schebgerag, "the torch of night;" also "the cup of the sun," &c.

† Franguestan—Circassia.

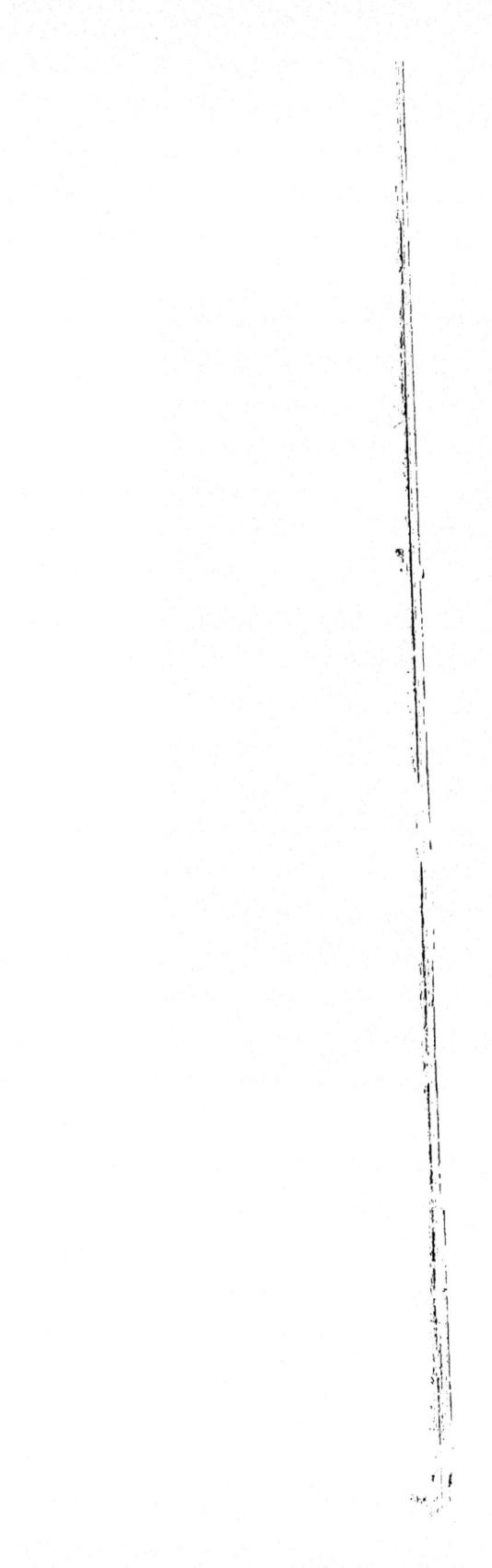

Painted by — Becanne. Engraved by S Sangster

THE NEXT FOND MOMENT SAW HER SEAT
HER FAIRY FORM AT SELIM'S FEET
"THIS ROSE TO CALM MY BROTHER'S CARES
"A MESSAGE FROM THE BULBUL BEARS
'IT SAYS TO-NIGHT HE WILL PROLONG
FOR SELIM'S EAR HIS SWEETEST SONG"

BRIDE OF ABYDOS.

Published by Smith, Elder & C° Cornhill London

SELIM AND ZULEIKA.

Painted by De Caisne.]   [Engraved by Sangster.

THE annexed engraving from a painting represents Zuleika's offering of the rose to Selim: a subject referring nearly to the same point of time as that illustrated by Mr. Richter in a former number.

In the present design, the vow is made: in the former, it is accepted.

After the unconscious Zuleika has uttered "the sacred oath" which binds her fate to that of her seeming brother, he conjures her to meet him during the night, at their favourite grotto in the Harem gardens, where, in former days, they had together spent their hours of childish mirth and youthful study.

The evening comes on wild and stormy; but true to her promise, she leaves her gorgeous bower, glowing with all the tributes of eastern luxury, and though trembling and starting at the hollow moaning of the tempest, she follows through the gloomy cypress groves the footsteps of the silent slave, who has been bribed to conduct her to Selim.

She finds their peaceful retreat furnished with arms, and Selim himself, throwing off his cloak, appears, not as a Pasha's son, but as the chief of a band of pirates. He informs her that he is not her brother, and Zuleika can scarcely check her tears, even when she finds that a dearer tie is to unite them in future, and that he has the power of making her the companion of his toils—the partaker of his triumphs.

> " With thee all toils are sweet, each clime hath charms,
> Earth—sea alike—our world within our arms."

She listens in mute and motionless distress to this recital, from which she learns her eternal separation, either from Selim, or from her father, against whose life her generous lover has voluntarily promised never to lift his arms, when distant voices and flashing torches announce betrayal and pursuit.

After a tender farewell to Zuleika, Selim, though despairing of escape, cleaves his way through his foes to the beach, to which the alarm of his pistol has summoned his faithful band. They struggle through the foam to his rescue,—in vain; for the lingering look which he turns towards the grotto of Zuleika, has made him a mark for the steady aim of Giaffer, and the same hand that drugged the bowl for the father, is embrued in the blood of the son.

He dies, not unrevenged, for Zuleika cannot survive her lover, and Giaffer is left in childless desolation.

> " Thou didst not see thy Selim fall!
> That fearful moment when he left the cave
> Thy heart grew chill:
> He was thy hope—thy joy—thy love—thine all—
> And the last thought on him thou couldst not save
> Sufficed to kill:
> Burst forth in one wild cry—and all was still."

Drawn by H Richter					Engraved by W Finden

AH! WERE I SEVER'D FROM THY SIDE,
WHERE WERE THY FRIEND—AND WHO MY GUIDE?
YEARS HAVE NOT SEEN, TIME SHALL NOT SEE
THE HOUR THAT TEARS MY SOUL FROM THEE'
BRIDE OF ABYDOS

Published by Smith Elder & C Cornhill London

THE BRIDE OF ABYDOS.

Painted by H. Richter.] [Engraved by W. Finden.

THE Pacha Giaffer, having destroyed his brother Abdallah by poison, is induced, by the intreaties of Haroun, one of his brother's slaves, to spare the life of Selim his infant nephew, and finally to adopt him as his son. Urged by some motives of shame, regret and remorse, or instigated by policy, as having no son of his own, Giaffer preserves the boy, but treats him with cruelty, and loads him with opprobrium. This harshness is increased when the dawning manhood of the youth mingles dread with his dislike; and the exceeding beauty of his daughter Zuleika, and her fondness for her supposed brother, increase his rage and jealousy beyond the bounds of concealment. It is at this period of the story that the poem opens. Giaffer informs Zuleika, in the presence of Selim, of his intention to marry her immediately to Osmyn Bey, and a scene of great beauty and tenderness follows, when the father has departed, and Selim is won from his melancholy reverie by the caresses of Zuleika, and by her voluntary promise never to marry against his wishes. Such is the subject of the accompanying engraving.

> " He lived — he breathed — he moved — he felt;
> He raised the maid from where she knelt,
> His name was gone — his keen eye shone
> With thoughts that long in darkness dwelt;

THE BRIDE OF ABYDOS.

With thoughts that burn — in rays that melt.
As the stream late conceal'd,
By the fringe of its willows,
When it rushes reveal'd
By the light of its billows.
As the bolt bursts on high
From the black cloud that bound it,
Flash'd the soul of that eye
Through the long lashes round it.
Now thou art mine, for ever mine,
With life to keep, and scarce with life resign.
Now thou art mine, that sacred oath,
Though sworn by one, has bound us both."

SHE THAT DAY HAD PASS'D
IN WATCHING ALL THAT HOPE PROCLAIM'D A MAST,
SADLY SHE SATE.

THE CORSAIR.

Published by Smith, Elder & Cº Cornhill London

THE CORSAIR.

Painted by Richter.] [Engraved by Dean.

MEDORA, the lonely, but beloved bride of the Corsair, is here represented, watching the dim horizon, to discover the distant sail that might announce the return of her husband, and sinking under the sickness of the heart, which arises from hope deferred. Her sufferings are finely described in the following passage:—

> " Oh! many a night, on this lone couch reclined,
> My dreaming fear with storms hath winged the wind,
> And deem'd the breath that faintly fann'd thy sail,
> The murmuring prelude of the ruder gale;
> Though soft, it seem'd the low prophetic dirge,
> That mourn'd thee floating on the savage surge:
> Still would I rise to rouse the beacon fire,
> Lest spies less true should let the blaze expire;
> And many a restless hour outwatched each star,
> And morning came—and still thou wert afar.
> Oh! how the chill blast on my bosom blew,
> And day broke dreary on my troubled view,
> And still I gazed and gazed, and not a prow
> Was granted to my tears—my truth—my vow!
> At length—'twas noon—I hail'd, and blest the mast
> That met my sight—it near'd—alas! it passed!"

Worn by this fever of the heart, and impatient of repose, during his last and fatal voyage she wanders over the midnight beach, reckless of the coming tide that dashes its spray over her garments, and warns her to depart:—

————————— " Impatience bore
At last her footsteps to the midnight shore,
And there she wandered heedless of the spray,
That dash'd her garments oft, and warned away·
She saw not—felt not this—nor dared depart,
Nor deem'd it cold—her chill was at her heart;
Till grew such certainty from that suspense—
His very sight had shock'd from life or sense!"

Drawn by H. Richter. Engraved by R. Baker.

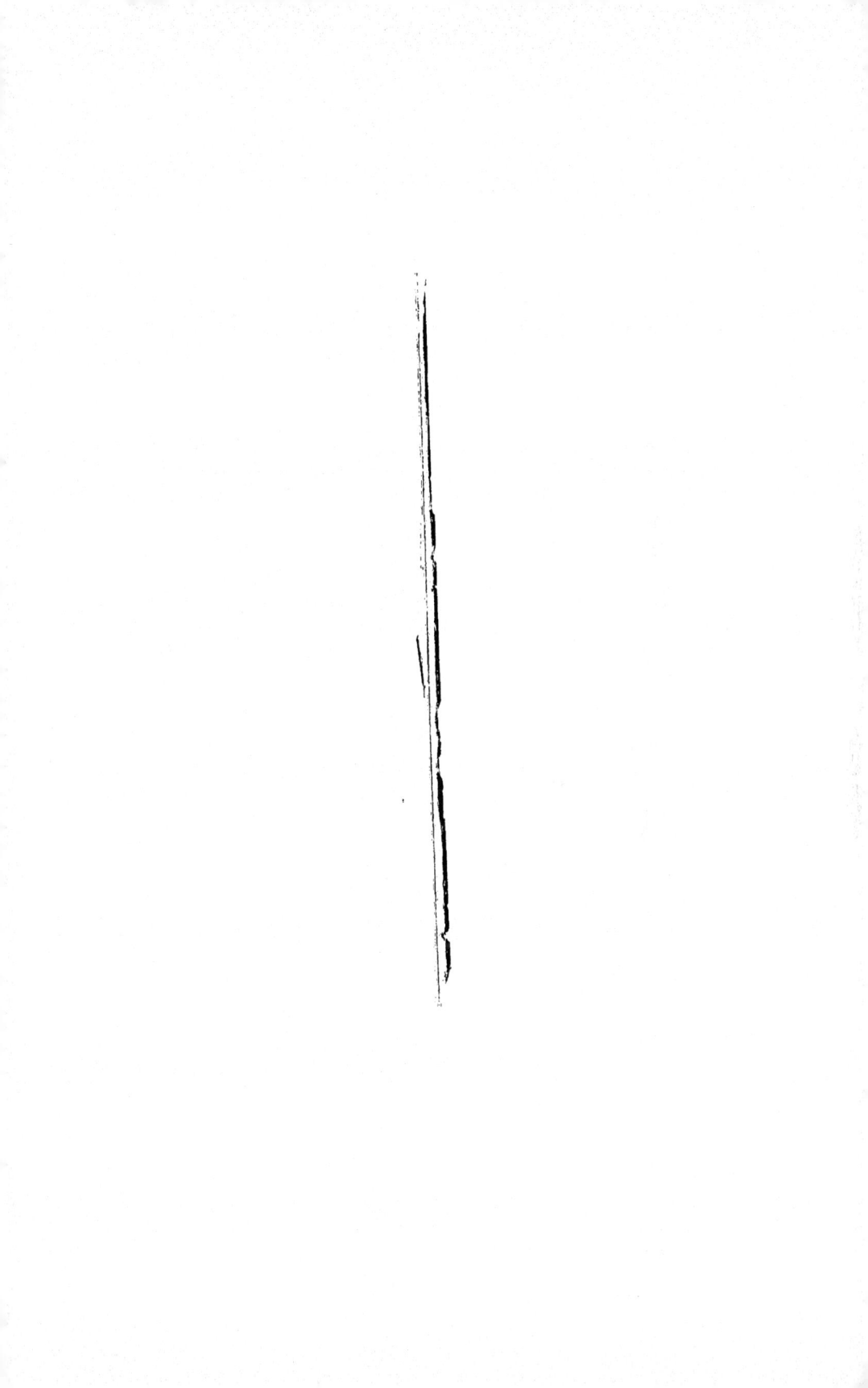

SEYD AND GULNARE.

Painted by Richter.]   [Engraved by Baker.

CONRAD has been obliged to leave his scarcely revisited bride, from the knowledge that his enemy Seyd intends, on the following night, to make an attack on his rocky retreat, and destroy his vessels and his fastnesses. The only chance of safety was to surprise his opponents, and burn the fleet by which their object was to be accomplished.

To make himself acquainted with the strength and resources of Seyd, Conrad disguises himself as a dervise, supposed to have escaped from the pirates, and is taken into the presence of Seyd for examination. Whilst the interrogatories proceed, and ere the suspicions of the Pasha are aroused, a blaze of light, illuminating sea and sky and the darkest recesses of the apartment, proclaims the destruction of his galleys; and the tyrant, starting up in a torrent of anger, calls on his slaves to secure the dervise. He has, however, cast away his robe and cap, and shines forth as a warrior armed for battle; whilst even Seyd, though brave, retreats before the fury of his blows. He joins his comrades, and they fire the city: but hearing the shrieks of the women in the blazing Harem, Conrad rushes at the head of his followers to their rescue, he himself saving from destruction the beautiful favourite of Seyd.

> "But who is she? whom Conrad's arms convey
> From reeking pile and combat's wreck away —
> Who, but the love of him he dooms to bleed?
> The Harem queen — but still the slave of Seyd!"

SEYD AND GULNARE.

The time thus humanely lost by the assailants is improved by the Pasha, in recalling his scattered soldiery. They return to the attack and are successful; Conrad is made prisoner, and the remnant of his followers escape to their vessels. To the captive, bound and wounded, a leech is sent, not in mercy, but to learn from the throbbing pulse if strength sufficient remains to prolong the prisoner's life till the morning ray shall witness his empalement.

> "Alone he sat—in solitude had scann'd
> His guilty bosom, but that breast he mann'd.
> One thought alone he could not—dared not meet—
> Oh, how these tidings will Medora greet!
> Then—only then—his clanking hands he raised,
> And strained with rage, the chain on which he gazed."

In the mean time the rescued beauty, Gulnare, is seated at the feet of her tyrant, whose cupidity she tries to tempt by representing the reported wealth of the captive, and the heavy ransom which might be extorted for his freedom.

She continues her remonstrances till his jealousy is aroused, and he answers—

> " And shall I then resign
> One day to him—the wretch already mine?
> Release my foe.—At whose remonstrance? thine!
> *   *   *   *   *
> I do mistrust thee, woman! and each word
> Of thine stamps truth on all suspicion heard.
> Borne in his arms through flames from yon Serai—
> Say, wert thou lingering there with him to fly?
> Thou need'st not answer—thy confession speaks
> Already reddening on thy guilty cheeks:
> Then lovely dame, bethink thee! and beware:
> 'Tis not *his* life alone may claim such care."

the example of Dryden, we scarcely believed that measure susceptible. It was yet to be proved that this, the most ponderous and stately verse in our language, could be accommodated to the variations of a tale of passion and of pity, and to all the breaks, starts and transitions of an adventurous and dramatic narration."

Painted by S.J.E. Jones. Engraved by W. Chevalier.

ROUSED BY THE SUDDEN SIGHT AT SUCH A TIME,
AND SOME FOREBODING THAT IT MIGHT BE CRIME,
HIMSELF UNHEEDED, WATCH'D THE STRANGER'S COURSE,
WHO REACH'D THE RIVER, BOUNDED FROM HIS HORSE,
AND FLING THENCE THE BURTHEN WHICH HE BORE,
HEAVED UP THE BANK, AND DASH'D IT FROM THE SHORE.
                                                    LARA.

Published by Smith Elder & Co Cornhill, London.

LARA.

Painted by Jones.] [Engraved by Chevallier.

LARA, a chief long absent from his own domain, returns at length, attended by a single page. Dark hints and surmises are thrown out against him by a noble, whom he encounters at a banquet, and who seems to be possessed of some knowledge of the manner in which Lara's time had been occupied during his prolonged absence.

This knight disappears, most opportunely for the reputation of Lara, when he should have come forward to substantiate the charges against him, and is never heard of after. A peasant, however, is witness to the concealment of a corpse on the same night, and the reader is left to draw his own conclusions.

The artist, who designed the accompanying plate, has adopted the opinion, that Lara, or at any event that a *man*, and not a *youth*, was employed in committing the body to the bosom of the silent waters. The impression on our mind has always been, that Kaled, the dark page, was the real culprit: for, considering Lara to be a continuation of the " Corsair," and Kaled of " Gulnare," it is difficult to suppose that the high-minded pirate, who refused to lift his arm against a sleeping enemy to save his own life, could, in the course of years, have deteriorated so far as to have become a midnight assassin, to preserve his reputation; whereas, with regard to Gulnare, one might say, as did the witty sceptic,* on hearing that Saint Denys had carried his head under his arm for two miles after decollation, " Je le crois bien, parceque ce n'est que le premier pas qui coute." When the attentive crowd expressed

> " Their marvel how the high-born Lara bore
> Such insult, from a stranger doubly sore,
> The colour of young Kaled went and came,
> The lip of ashes, and the cheek of flame;
> And o'er his brow the dampening heart-drops threw
> The sickening iciness of that cold dew,
> That rises as the busy bosom sinks
> With heavy thoughts from which reflection shrinks.
> Yes—there be things which we must dream and dare,
> And execute ere thought be half aware;
> Whate'er might Kaled's be, it was enow
> To seal his lip, but agonise his brow."

* Saint Denys was the first bishop of Paris, about the year 245, and the legend of his carrying his head was once as steadfastly believed as any primary article of faith. On one occasion, a friar was relating it to the infidel and witty Madame du Deffand, and, trying to moderate the miracle to what he suspected to be the measure of her faith, said, that the Saint certainly found it very difficult *at first*: " Je le crois bien, mon Père," replied the lady :—" dans ce cas, ce n'est que le premier pas qui coute."

FRANCESCA.

WHAT DID THAT SUDDEN SOUND BESPEAK?
HE TURN'D TO THE LEFT — IS HE SURE OF SIGHT?
THERE SAT A LADY, YOUTHFUL AND BRIGHT!

THE SIEGE OF CORINTH.

FRANCESCA.

Painted by W. Penley.]   [Engraved by R. Staines.

THE siege of Corinth, which Lord Byron has peopled with " beings of his thought, reflected," took place at the beginning of the eighteenth century, when Cournougi, the grand vizier of Achemet III., recovered the Peloponnesus from the Venetians.

Alp, the hero of the tale, is by birth a noble Venetian, whom state intrigues had banished from his native city, and whom a burning sense of injuries unavenged has induced to assume the turban, in the hope of teaching his ungrateful countrymen,

> " How great their loss
> In him who triumph'd o'er the Cross,
> 'Gainst which he rear'd the Crescent high,
> And battled to avenge or die."

But not for vengeance alone did the renegade lead his hostile troops against Corinth. A maiden, loving and beloved, sought by, and refused to him in happier hours, is secluded within the walls, whom he hopes to obtain without the consent of her inexorable father. On the night preceding the attack which Alp is to lead against the devoted city, he wanders out over the midnight landscape, amongst the drooping banners and silent tents of the besieging army, which are described with that vivid appearance of reality, in which Lord Byron was so unrivalled in poetry, as was Scott in prose.

The cold round moon shining over innumerable outspread tents, the azure air, and almost waveless ocean;—the thousand sleepers spread along the shore, whilst Delphi's hill, rises high with her eternal snow in the distance, as described in this exquisite passage, have all the truth of a perfect picture, with an additional power of which painting is unsusceptible; for sound is added, and the stillness broken by the long sad cry of the Muezzin's voice calling to prayer; that voice that falls dreary and ominous on the ear even of the besiegers, and strikes the inhabitants of the devoted city as a warning prophetic of its fall.

Alp seats himself at the base of some ruined columns, and passes his hand over his brow in troubled and fevered thought. A thrilling whisper is at his ear, like the sound of a passing breeze; but the long grass is unshaken, and the ocean unruffled,

> " He looked to the banners—each flag lay still,
> So did the leaves on Cithæron's hill,
> And he felt not a breath come over his cheek;
> What did that sudden sound bespeak?
> He turned to the left—is he sure of the sight?
> There sate a lady, youthful and bright!"

The appearance, which is that of his Francesca, reproaches him with his apostacy, and warns him of future judgment unless he repent.

> "There is a light cloud by the moon—
> 'Tis passing, and will pass full soon:—
> If, by the time its vapoury sail,
> Hath ceased her shaded orb to veil,
> Thy heart within thee is not changed,
> Then God and man are both avenged;
> Dark will thy doom be, darker still
> Thine immortality of ill.
>   *   *   *   *
> He looked upon it earnestly,
> Without an accent of reply;
> He watched it passing; it is flown:
> Full on his eye the clear moon shone,
> And thus he spake—' Whate'er my fate,
> ' I am no changeling—'tis too late.' "

Painted by E. C. Wood.   Engraved by W. Finden.

SHE LISTENS — BUT NOT FOR THE NIGHTINGALE —
THOUGH HER EAR EXPECTS AS SOFT A TALE
THERE GLIDES A STEP THROUGH THE FOLIAGE THICK,
AND HER CHEEK GROWS PALE — AND HER HEART BEATS QUICK
THERE WHISPERS A VOICE THROUGH THE RUSTLING LEAVES,
AND HER BLUSH RETURNS, AND HER BOSOM HEAVES

PARISINA.

Published by Smith Elder & Co. Cornhill, London.

PARISINA.

Painted by E. C. Wood.] [Engraved by Finden.

THE opening stanzas of Parisina contain a description of twilight, or rather of the union between twilight and night, which is eminently beautiful; and which, though soft and voluptuous, is tinged with that shade of sorrow, which gives character and harmony to the whole poem.

The annexed design is intended to illustrate the following passage:

> "But it is not to list to the waterfall
> That Parisina leaves her hall.
>   *   *
> She listens—but not for the nightingale—
> Though her ear expects as soft a tale.
> There glides a step through the foliage thick,
> And her cheek turns pale—and her heart beats quick.
> There whispers a voice through the rustling leaves,
> And her blush returns, and her bosom heaves:
> A moment more—and they shall meet—
> 'Tis past—her lover 's at her feet."

Parisina had been betrothed to Hugo, the natural son of Azo, Prince of Estè. Azo saw, and coveted her beauty; and reproaching his son for the stain of his birth, which, he said, rendered him unworthy the possession of so rich a treasure, he himself wedded the promised bride of the indignant Hugo. The passion, which was not only innocent, but praiseworthy in its commencement, the unhappy lovers could not control, when a change of circumstances had rendered it criminal. Parisina mutters in her dreams words of tenderness; and, whilst Azo

> " Could in very fondness weep,
> O'er her who loves him even in sleep,"

she couples with those endearing tones, the name of the lover from whom she had parted in the twilight hour, whose cherished memory still haunts her sleeping fancy. Azo draws his sabre, with the intention of wiping out his dishonour on the instant, but

> " Could not slay a thing so fair,
> At least, not smiling, sleeping, there."

In the morning, he learns the tale of his disgrace from the lips of the long confiding attendants, who are anxious to exculpate themselves, by transferring the guilt, the shame, and the punishment to the principals. The guilty step-mother and hapless son are instantly summoned to the judgment-seat:

> " And the crowd in a speechless circle gather,
> To see the son fall by the doom of the father."

Drawn by H. Richter. Engraved by W. Chevalier.

AND THEREFORE BOW'D HE FOR A SPACE
AND PASS'D HIS SHAKING HAND ALONG
HIS EYE, TO VEIL IT FROM THE THRONG
WHILE HUGO RAISED HIS CHAINED HANDS,
AND FOR A BRIEF DELAY DEMANDS
HIS FATHERS EAR
PARISINA.

Published by Smith Elder & Cº Cornhill London.

PARISINA.

Painted by Richter.] [Engraved by Chevallier.

THE grand part of this poem is that which describes the defence of Hugo, and the execution of that rival son; and in which, though there is no pomp, either of language or of sentiment, and though every thing is conceived and expressed with the utmost simplicity and directness, there is a spirit of pathos and poetry to which it would not be easy to find many parallels.

The following extract from Gibbon will prove that, unhappily, fact was the foundation of the tale: Lord Byron substituting *Azo* for Nicholas, as more metrical.

" Under the reign of Nicholas III. Ferrara was polluted with a domestic tragedy. By the testimony of an attendant, and his own observation, the Marquis of Estè discovered the incestuous loves of his wife Parisina, and his natural son Hugo, a beautiful and valiant youth. They were beheaded in the castle by the sentence of a father and husband, who published his shame, and survived their execution. He was unfortunate if they were guilty; if they were innocent, he was still more unfortunate; nor is there any possible situation, in which I can sincerely approve the last act of the justice of a parent."

" Ferrara is much decayed and depopulated," says Lord Byron, in one of his letters; "but the castle still exists entire; and I saw the court where Parisina and Hugo were beheaded, according to the annal of Gibbon."

In the poem, the fate of Parisina is left doubtful; but the following statement, in Frizzi's History of Ferrara, confirms the account of Gibbon.

"It was, then, in the prisons of the castle, and exactly in those frightful dungeons, beneath the chamber called the Aurora, that, on the night of the 21st of May, were beheaded, first Hugo, and then Parisina. Zoese, he that accused her, conducted the latter under his arm to the place of punishment. She, all along, fancied she was to be thrown into a pit, and asked, at every step, if she was yet come to the spot? She was told, that her punishment was the axe. She inquired what was become of Hugo, and received for answer, that he was already dead; at the which, sighing grievously, she exclaimed, 'Now then, I wish not myself to live;' and, being come to the block, she stripped herself with her own hands of all her ornaments, and, wrapping a cloth round her head, submitted to the fatal stroke, which terminated the cruel scene.

"The marquis kept watch the whole of that dreadful night, and, as he was walking backwards and forwards, inquired, of the captain of the castle, if Hugo was dead yet? Who answered him, 'Yes.' He then gave himself up to the most desperate lamentations, exclaiming, 'Oh! that I too were dead, since I have been hurried on to resolve thus against my own Hugo!' and then, gnawing with his teeth a cane which he had in his hand, he passed the rest of the night in sighs and tears, calling frequently upon his own dear Hugo."

Drawn by J. P. Davis. Engraved by J. Goodyear.

VENETIAN WOMEN WEEP, AND SO THEY ARE
PARTICULARLY SEEN FROM A BALCONY,
(FOR BEAUTY'S SOMETIMES BEST SET OFF AFAR)
AND THERE, JUST LIKE A HEROINE OF GOLDONI,
THEY PEEP FROM OUT THE BLIND, OR O'ER THE BAR,
AND, TRUTH TO SAY, THEY'RE MOSTLY VERY PRETTY,
AND RATHER LIKE TO SHOW IT, MORE'S THE PITY.

BEPPO

Published by Smith Elder & Cº Cornhill, London.

BEPPO.

<small>Painted by Davis.]　　　　　　　　　　　　　　　[Engraved by Goodyear.</small>

XI.

"They 've pretty faces yet, those same Venetians,
　Black eyes, arch'd brows, and sweet expressions still;
Such as of old were copied from the Grecians,
　In ancient arts by moderns mimick'd ill;
And like so many Venuses of Titian's
　(The best 's at Florence — see it, if ye will),
They look when leaning over the balcony,
Or stepp'd from out a picture by Giorgione,

XII.

Whose tints are truth and beauty at their best."

GIORGIONE, and Titian, who for some time copied his style, seem to have been the only painters who excited, in any great degree, the admiration of Lord Byron. Giorgione was especially his favourite, and deservedly so, from the grace, dignity, expression, and truth of character, which distinguish his compositions; to which may be added, the beauty with which he invests his female heads, a charm more likely to attract one of the uninitiated than even higher qualities in painting. There are very few specimens of this master in England, and, from his early death at thirty-four, his paintings are rare even on the Continent. Two beautiful compositions by Giorgione adorn the collection of Mr. Hope, in Duchess Street; one the head of a woman, whose majesty and loveliness realize all that imagination can desire.

"I know nothing of pictures myself and care almost as little; but to me there are none like the Venetian — above all, Giorgione." — B. LETTERS, 1817.

THE GONDOLA.

LAURA WAS BLOOMING STILL, HAD MADE THE BEST
OF TIME, AND TIME RETURND THE COMPLIMENT
AND TREATED HER GENTEELY, SO THAT, DRESSD
SHE LOOK'D EXTREMELY WELL WHERE ER SHE WENT
A PRETTY WOMAN IS A WELCOME GUEST
AND LAURAS BROW A FROWN HAD RARELY BENT
INDEED SHE SHONE ALL SMILES AND SEEM'D TO FLATTER
MANKIND WITH HER BLACK EYES FOR LOOKING AT HER —

BEPPO. STANZA

Published by Smith Elder & Co Cornhill London

THE GONDOLA.

Painted by Richter.]   [Engraved by E. Finden.

The lovely freight, with which Mr. Richter has adorned his Gondola, so attracts the eyes of the spectator, that he forgets the angular and unpleasing form of the vessel. Were it not for tender and poetical recollections, that have lingered round Gondolas ever since the days of Shakspeare to those of Byron, we should pronounce them to be exceedingly ugly and ungraceful.

> " Didst ever see a Gondola ? For fear
> You should not, I'll describe it you exactly:
> 'Tis a long cover'd boat that's common here,
> Carved at the prow, built lightly, but compactly;
> Rowed by two rowers, each called ' Gondolier,'
> It glides along the water looking blackly,
> Just like a coffin clapt in a canoe,
> Where none can make out what you say or do."

" In Venice," says a celebrated traveller, " the Gondoliers know by heart long passages from Ariosto and Tasso, and often chaunt them with a peculiar melody. I entered a Gondola by moonlight; one singer placed himself forwards, and the other aft, and thus proceeded to Saint Georgeo. One began the song; when he had ended his strophe, the other took up the lay, and so continued the song alternately. Throughout the whole of it, the same notes invariably returned, but according to the subject matter of the strophe, they laid a greater, or a smaller stress, sometimes on one, and sometimes on another note; and indeed changed the enunciation of the whole strophe, as the object of the poem altered.

"On the whole, however, the sounds were hoarse and screaming: they seemed, in the manner of rude uncivilized men, to make the excellency of their singing in the force of their voice; and so far from receiving delight from this scene (shut up, as I was, in the box of the Gondola), I found myself in a very unpleasant situation. Accordingly we got upon the shore, leaving one of the singers in the Gondola, while the other went to the distance of some hundred paces. Here the scene was properly introduced. The strong declamatory, and, as it were, shrieking sound, met the ear from far, and called forth the attention; the quickly succeeding transitions, which necessarily required to be sung in a lower tone, seemed like the plaintive strain succeeding the vociferations of emotion or of pain. The other, who listened attentively, immediately began where the former left off, answering him in milder or more vehement notes, according as the purport of the strophe required. The sleepy canals, the lofty buildings, the deep shadows of the few Gondolas, that moved hither and thither, increased the striking peculiarity of the scene; and amid all these circumstances, it is easy to confess the character of this wonderful harmony."

"'Tis sweet to hear,
At midnight on the blue and moonlit deep,
The song and oar of Adria's Gondolier,
By distance mellowed, o'er the waters sweep."

LONDON: PRINTED BY STEWART AND MURRAY, OLD BAILEY.

"SIR," (QUOTH THE TURK) "'TIS NO MISTAKE AT ALL
THAT LADY IS *MY WIFE*!" MUCH WONDER PAINTS
THE LADY'S CHANGING CHEEK, AS WELL IT MIGHT,
BUT WHERE AN ENGLISHWOMAN SOMETIMES FAINTS,
ITALIAN FEMALES DON'T DO SO OUTRIGHT

BEPPO.

Published by Smith, Elder & Cº Cornhill, London.

BEPPO.

Painted by Richter.] [Engraved by Ryall.

The charm of this poem consists in the playfulness and gaiety of the style. There is little story, few incidents, and not much delineation of character in the actors. Of the latter, Laura is the most elaborated and the most amusing. She refutes too, by her individuality, the sweeping charge brought against all the female characters of Byron, of resemblance to each other. This poem, though published anonymously, rose immediately, from its talent and novelty, to a degree of popularity, precedented only by the success of Byron's earlier poems; though the scrupulous were, even then, scandalized at the levity with which the author spoke of some actions as follies, which they had been accustomed to consider as crimes.

Laura, a pretty woman of "a certain age," was wedded to a merchant trading to Aleppo, Beppo by name, to whom she made a tender and devoted wife, till, on one fatal voyage, his prolonged absence tried her patience beyond the bounds of feminine endurance.

" And Laura waited long, and wept a little,
And thought of wearing weeds, as well she might;
She almost lost all appetite for victual,
And could not sleep with ease alone at night;
She deemed the window frames and shutters brittle
Against a daring house-breaker or sprite,
And so she thought it prudent to connect her
With a vice-husband, *chiefly* to protect her."

The chosen cavalier is an "arbiter elegantiarum" amongst beaux and belles,—a Venetian exquisite,—moreover one of those

> "Lovers of the good old school,
> Who always grow more constant as they cool."

One evening, as Laura and the Count are enjoying the pleasures of the Carnival, the lady is both flattered and amused by the fixed gaze of a figure dressed as a Turk; and, on their return home, they find themselves preceded by the Mussulman, who, in reply to the haughty interrogatories of the Count, claims Laura as his wife! This occasions some little confusion at first; but nothing can be more amicably arranged than the conclusion: for they all reside in perfect harmony, and though

> "Laura sometimes put him in a passion,
> I've heard the count and he were always friends."

The philosophy of this arrangement reminds us of the countryman, mentioned by Steele, who when at the representation of the "Fatal Marriage," looked round with astonishment at the sympathy of the audience with the shame, grief, and agony of Isabella, on the return of her first husband: exclaiming, "Well! now let every man have his mare again!" A view of the question which would, doubtless, have saved much misery and bloodshed.

Painted by Richter.] [Engraved by Staines.

———

THE subject of this poem, which is so wild and improbable, that its incidents seem more like the sequence of a troubled dream, than a matter of fact, is founded on the following circumstance. A Polish gentleman, named Mazeppa, was educated as page to John Casimir, at whose court he became imbued with some taste for elegant literature. It would seem that the culture of his morals kept not pace with the improvement of his intellect; for at an early age he was detected in an intrigue with a lady, whose husband adopted the following singular mode of vengeance. He caused the young offender to be fastened, naked, on the back of a wild Ukraine horse, which bore the helpless rider, half dead with fatigue and hunger, ack to its native wilds. Rescued from death by some peasants, the superiority of Mazeppa's knowledge gave him great importance amongst the Cossacks; and his reputation augmenting each day, obliged the Czar to make him prince of the Ukraine. Lord Byron has told the fearful speed of the wild horse with his usual power, and lingered over the love, which terminated so disastrously, with more than his usual tenderness. Mazeppa is himself the relater, when age has blunted the acute remembrance of his sufferings, and furrowed his brow, and stiffened his limbs, and dimmed all but the vision of youth and beauty, which rises in unchanged brightness at the name of Theresa.

The artist has portrayed the scene, in which Mazeppa first suspects that his passion is returned, from the lady's indifference as to the result of the game at which they are engaged; whilst she continues to play

> "As if her will
> Yet bound her to the place, though not
> That her's might be the winning lot."

Drawn by H. Richter. Engraved by H.C Shenton.

SHE AS HE GAZED WITH GRATEFUL WONDER PRESSED
HER SHELTERED LOVE TO HER IMPASSIONED BREAST,
AND SUITED TO HER SOFT CARESSES TOLD
AN OLDEN TALE OF LOVE.   *THE ISLAND*

Published by Smith Elder & Co Cornhill London

THE ISLAND.

Painted by Richter.] [Engraved by Shenton.

In 1789 a band of young mutineers, headed by Christian, took possession of the Bounty, and, as the captain dreamed in his cabin of the prosperous termination of his voyage, and the joys of home, he was rudely seized, and forced into an open boat, whilst his crew steered back to Otaheite.

In this wild paradise of nature, where health, beauty, and plenty surround the fortunate inhabitants:—health unbroken—beauty almost universal, and plenty that "tasks not one laborious hour:" these

> "Men without country, who, too long estranged,
> Had found no native home, or found it changed."

for many months enjoyed a happy refuge.

But the hand of vengeance, though delayed, is not withdrawn. A strange sail seen in the offing proves to be a vessel sent in search of the mutineers, and all prepare for resistance till death. They are crushed, dispersed, or slain; or survive, wounded and faint, to envy those who have fallen. Their new allies in vain oppose their naked bodies in defence of their guests; for what can avail the club or spear, or the strength of a Hercules against the "sulphury charm"—that destroys the warrior ere his strength can be made available.

Drooping and dispirited, Christian collects his little band behind a jutting crag. He grieves for all, but most his heart is torn for the fate of young Torquil, "the fair-haired offspring of the Hebrides," who is leaning faint and wounded against the projecting rock.

> "And is it thus?" he cried, "unhappy boy!
> And thee, too, *thee*—my madness must destroy!"

As he speaks, the plash of hostile oars gives notice that this last retreat is insecure, and Neuha, the young bride of Torquil, beckoning the natives round her in their canoes, embarks Christian and his surviving comrades in one proa, whilst she herself takes the charge of Torquil in another.

The light proas dart along the bay; swiftly they fly; swiftly are they followed by the hostile boats: at length they separate to baffle pursuit, and Neuha, ordering her rowers to assist Christian, steers her course to a desert rock rising in the midst of the ocean. By this timely aid, the light canoe of Christian darts forward like a shooting star, and the pursuers turn their course after the lovers. Nothing is visible but the stern inexorable face of the crag, and Torquil, half upbraiding, asks if Neuha has brought him there to die? The crew now call on him to surrender, but Neuha, bidding him follow her, leaps into the waves, and they disappear, leaving not a trace "rebubbling on the main," to betray their course. The wondering sailors believe their disappearance to be supernatural; whilst after diving deeper and deeper, the lovers rise at length to a central realm of earth, which, though undecked by field, or tree, or sky, the prophetic love of Neuha has stored with all the hoarded luxuries of that happy climate.

> "A pine torch pile to keep undying light,
> And she herself, as beautiful as night,
> To fling her shadowy spirit o'er the scene,
> And make their subterranean world serene."

Drawn by H. Corbould.   Engraved by J Romney

MAN   OH GOD' IF IT BE THUS AND *THOU*
ART NOT A MADNESS AND A MOCKERY,
I YET MIGHT BE MOST HAPPY — I WILL CLASP THEE
AND WE AGAIN WILL BE

MANFRED

Published by Smith Elder & Cº Cornhill London

i

MANFRED.

Painted by H. Corbould.] [Engraved by J. Romney.

MANFRED is represented by the poet, as a being estranged from all human creatures, indifferent to all human sympathies, and dwelling in the magnificent solitude of the Central Alps, where he holds communion only with the spirits he invokes by his sorceries, and with the fearful memory of the being he has loved and destroyed.

It is scarcely possible to read this beautiful poem without recurring to a production somewhat similar in another country; and in all that concerns their attachment to their several victims, how infinitely superior is the Manfred of Byron, to the Faustus of Goethe! It is the difference between the devotion of a spirit, and the appetite of an animal.

The attraction which Faustus feels towards Margaret is merely physical. She captivates simply by her youth and beauty, and by the innocence which he seeks to destroy. There is, there can be, in her mind, no conception of, no intercourse with, the mighty intellect of her lord. But of Astarte it is said—

> "She had the same lone thoughts and wanderings,
> The quest of hidden knowledge, and a mind
> To comprehend the universe."

If sin, sorrow, and death are equally the result, how much less gross are the motives of action in Manfred!

Margaret is no sooner won than neglected, and left to pine

away her days in solitude, and finally to conceal her crime by murder.

> " My peace is gone! my heart is broken, I never shall find it more.
> I gaze from the window for him! I go from the house to look out for him.
> His stately step! his noble stature! his smile! the fire of his eye;
> The magic flow of his words, the pressure of his hand! and ah, his kiss!
> My peace is gone! my heart is broken, I never shall find it more."

But the love so vividly portrayed in Manfred, is a feeling unslumbering, and undying, even in the misery, insanity, desolation and death by which it is accompanied. The cause of his unceasing remorse is so dimly shadowed forth, that we shrink from our own suspicions of the nature of the crime that bears so fearful a punishment. The actors in this drama have a preternatural character, which removes them equally from our sympathy and reprobation.

Goethe has given more of human interest to his heroine. Astarte, though with such sad and solemn beauty on her " airie brow," is as unreal as the witch of the Alps. She comes from the grave to tell of future judgments; and we feel an oppressive and breathless awe, as if an apparition were really present. Margaret is a living and tangible creature: we see her led by her mother's hand to the church, or watching by the cradle of her infant sister, or gazing with childish curiosity and delight at the unexpected jewels, provided by her tempter.

The scene portrayed by the designer, represents Manfred in his study, when, having invoked his attendant spirits, one assumes the form of Astarte.

Painted by H. Howard, R.A. Engraved by F. Bacon.

                                           SON OF EARTH!
With I know thee and the powers which give thee power
              WHAT WOULDST THOU WITH ME?
Man. TO LOOK UPON THY BEAUTY — NOTHING FURTHER.
                                                    MANFRED.

MANFRED.

Painted by Howard.] [Engraved by Bacon

A GOOD picture may be considered to be a kind of half-way house between the fiction of a poet's brain and the sternness of reality.

> "Such sights as youthful poets dream
> At Summer eve by haunted stream"

would be lost for ever to the generality of mankind, who are unpoetical, unless some spirit, kindred to the poet's, strive to catch the glorious pageant ere it melt away, and to body it forth in colours instead of sentences, substituting the painter's palette for the poet's vocabulary.

What a mixture of sternness and beauty in the countenance of the witch! How well her position seems to express motion without bodily effort,—the gliding of a spirit! Mr. Howard has wisely avoided the difficulty of representing her "charms" as of an "unearthly stature," which, however in accordance with the grandeur of the Alpine scenery around her, would have reduced the figure of Manfred to the proportions of a pigmy.

A poet, for whom Lord Byron generally expressed the greatest, but most undeserved, contempt, has conveyed his notion of spiritual grandeur in a manner somewhat similar to that of the noble author. The resemblance is probably accidental; though Byron allowed "Hyperion" to be "a fine monument, and likely to preserve the name" of the unfortunate Keats.

> " She was a goddess of the infant world;
> By her in stature the tall Amazon
> Had stood a pigmy's height:"
> " Her face was large as that of Memphian sphinx,
> *Pedestal'd* haply in a palace court,
> When sages look'd to Egypt for their lore."

It may be, that both poets unconsciously drew upon their scholastic recollections; and that the " umbra Creusæ," "nota major imago," was the origin of both passages.

Painted by Richard Westall, R.A. Engraved by W. Finden.

Doge – WHEN SHE SHAKES OFF THIS TEMPORARY DEATH,
I SHALL BE WITH THE ETERNAL
ONE LOOK' – HOW COLD HER HAND' – AS COLD AS MINE
SHALL BE ERE SHE RECOVERS – GENTLY TEND HER,
AND TAKE MY LAST THANKS. –

MARINO FALIERO.

Published by Smith Elder & Co Cornhill London

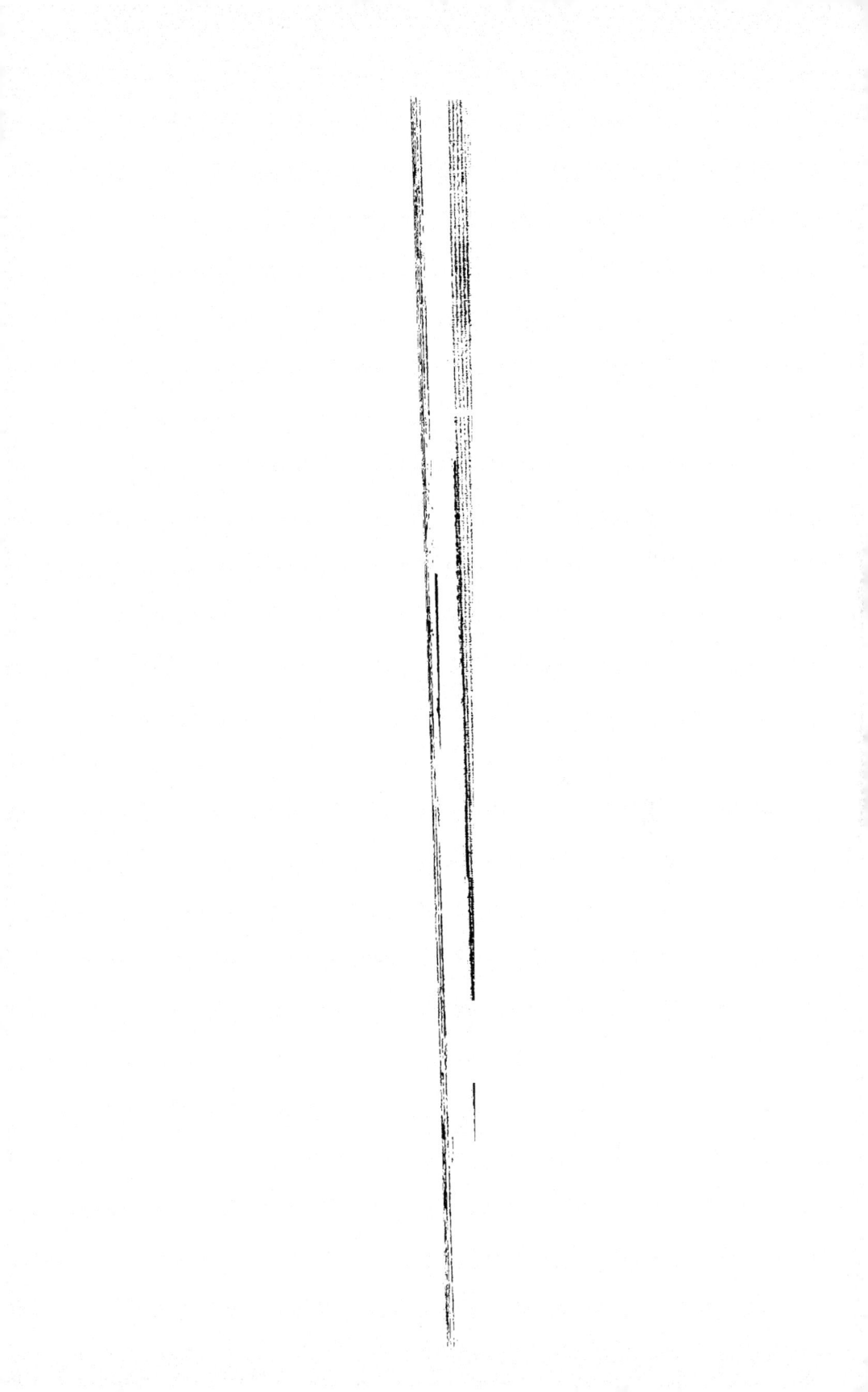

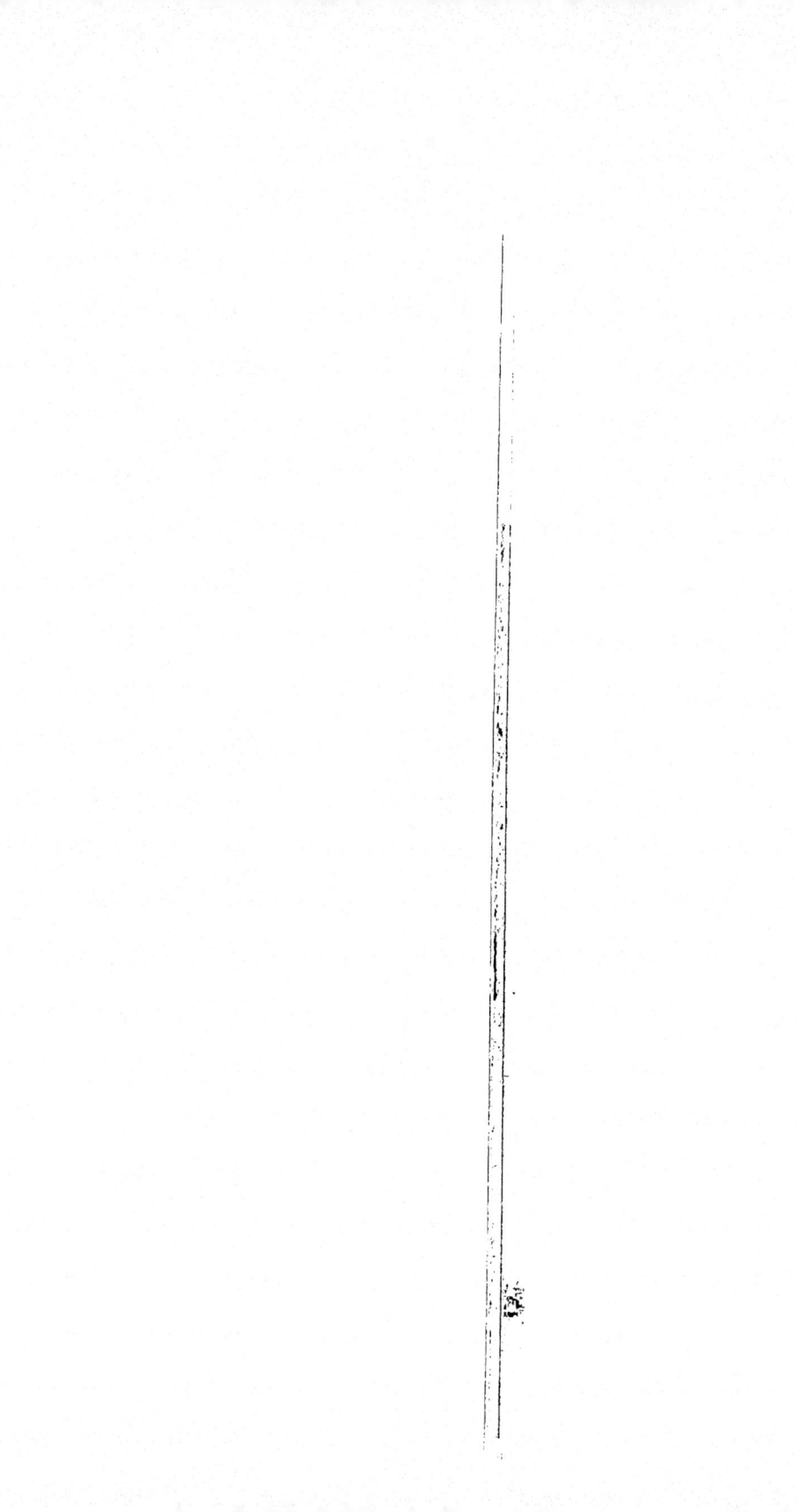

MARINO FALIERO.

[Painted by Westall.]   [Engraved by W. Finden]

THE scene chosen by Mr. Westall for the illustration of Marino Faliero, is the parting of the Doge from his wife, previous to his execution. The story on which the tragedy is founded, is authentic; and it is necesssary to remember this, to reconcile the mind to its seeming improbability. The young, and beautiful, and virtuous Duchess has been libelled by the wantonness of a young patrician; and, on account of the inadequate punishment inflicted by the Council of Forty for this offence, the Doge conspires against the state of which he is the head. The treason is discovered, "sentence is pronounced, a brief hour is permitted for the last devotions, and then—still robed in his ducal gown, and wearing the diadem—preceded with all the pomp of his station, from which he is to be degraded in the moment only before the blow be struck,—Marino Faliero is led solemnly to the Giant's Staircase, at the summit of which he had been crowned. On that spot he is to expiate his offence against the majesty of the Venetian State. His wife struggles to accompany him to the dreadful spot, but she faints, and he leaves her on the marble pavement, forbidding them to raise her, until all had been accomplished with himself." There

MARINO FALIERO.

is much beauty and pathos in the last address of the Doge to his wife:—

> "Then, farewell, Angiolina!—one embrace—
> Forgive the old man who hath been to thee
> A fond, but fatal husband.
>   —In one hour
> I have uprooted all my former life,
> And outlived everything, except thy heart,
> The pure, the good, the gentle, which will oft
> With unimpair'd but not a clamorous grief
> Still keep—Thou turn'st so pale!—Alas! she faints,
> She has no breath, no pulse!—Guards! lend your aid—
> I cannot leave her thus, and yet 'tis better,
> Since every lifeless moment spares a pang."

Drawn by H. Richter.   Engraved by E. J. Portbury.

Japhet. 'THEY ARE GONE!' THEY HAVE DISAPPEAR'D AMIDST THE ROAR
OF THE FORSAKEN WORLD, AND NEVER MORE,
WHETHER THEY LIVE, OR DIE WITH ALL EARTH'S LIFE,
NOW NEAR ITS LAST, CAN AUGHT RESTORE
ANAH UNTO THESE EYES.
                                               HEAVEN & EARTH

Published by Smith, Elder & C. Cornhill London.

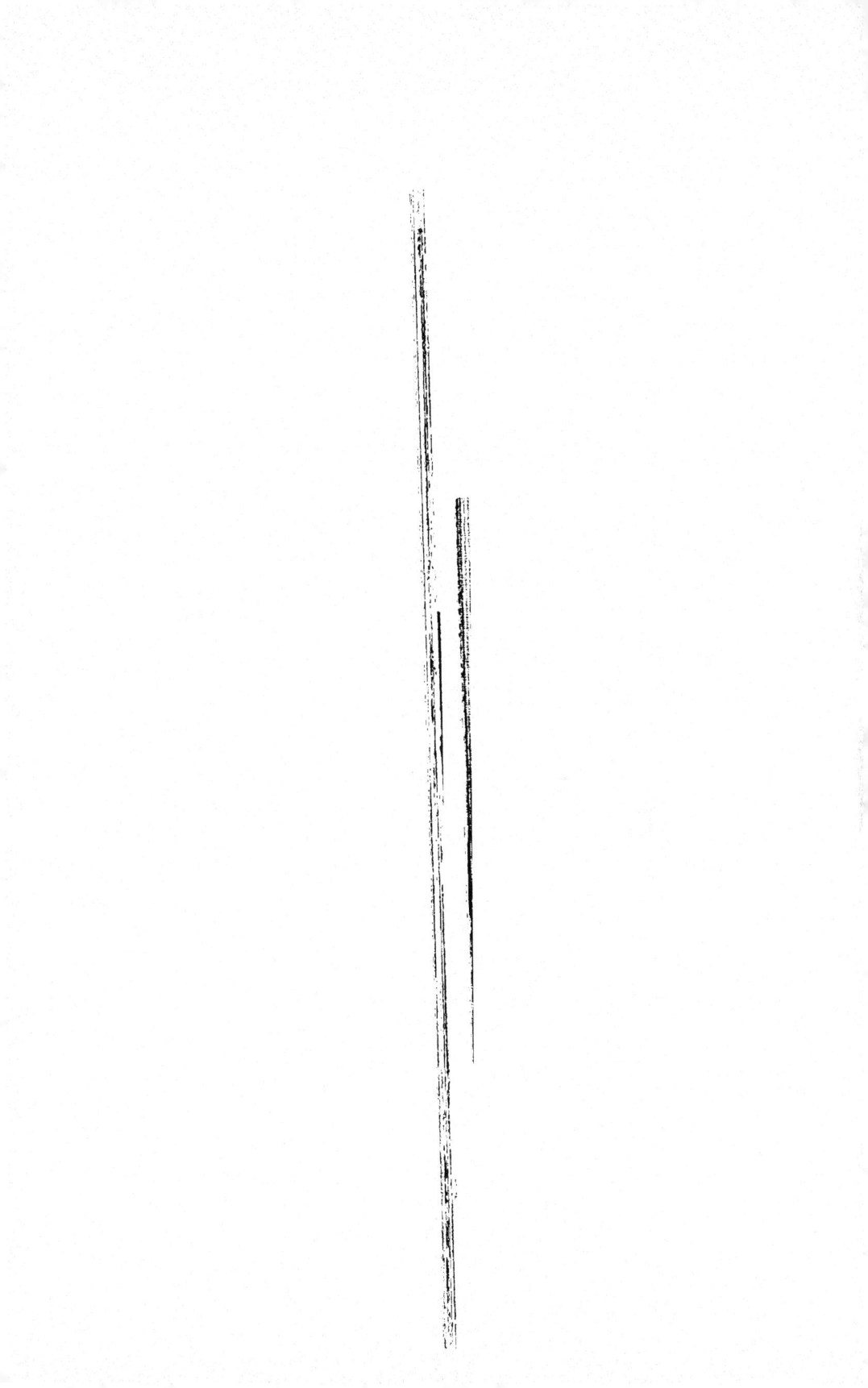

HEAVEN AND EARTH.

Painted by Richter.] [Engraved by Portbury.

THIS is a wild and solemn, but a very painful poem: most painful, because it engages all our sympathies, and arouses all our terrors. It represents God, as the God of the whirlwind and the tempest,—the God, not of mercy but of vengeance,—the destroyer, not the preserver of the beautiful universe. Our conviction of the truth of the leading features of this drama adds to its power. Not only have the Holy Writings impressed the reality of the deluge on our conviction from infancy, but every feature in the present aspect of nature confirms its truth. The rocky ravine, bearing traces of the torrent's violence, though waters rush no longer down its bed: mighty forests buried deep below the surface of the earth: "the little shells of ocean's least things," embedded amongst roots of mountain flowers: the fossil mammoth dug from his age-enduring tomb: all speak a voice intelligible to the sceptic as to the christian.

The dreary feeling conveyed by this poem arises also from the circumstance, that we see the punishment impending, with only a general notion of the sin that has caused it, and we forget the guilt in anticipation of the suffering.

We regard the Being, on whom we depend for all happiness, in his inexplicable wisdom dealing with the innocent as with the guilty: visiting the sins of the parents on the children, and overwhelming all his works in one universal ruin.

There are few hearts that will not respond to the mother's appeal to Japhet.

A mother (offering her infant to Japhet,)

> "Oh let this child embark!
> I brought him forth in woe,
>   But thought it joy
> To see him to my bosom clinging so.
>   Why was he born?
>   What hath he done—
>   My unwean'd son—
> To move Jehovah's wrath or scorn?
> What is there in this milk of mine, that death
> Should stir all heaven and earth up to destroy
>   My boy,
> And roll the waters o'er his placid breath?
> Save him, thou seed of Seth!"

Little interest is felt for the principal individuals in this Mystery. Here, as in the storms of Salvator and Poussin, it is the general aspect of nature that fixes the attention; and though human creatures are seen struggling against the violence of the elements, they are too insignificant to interfere with the grandeur of Nature's strife. Thus, in this sublime poem, we hear the din of the rising waters: the rushing of the mighty winds: the laughter of the exulting demons: the trembling earth, and the lowering sky announce the dissolution of nature, and we mourn with Japhet over the universal destruction, more than we sympathise with his unhappy love.

At the conclusion of the poem the angel-lovers snatch their mortal maidens from the coming doom:

> "We will bear ye far
> To some untroubled star,
> Where thou and Anah shall partake our lot:
> And if thou dost not weep for thy lost earth,
> Our forfeit heaven shall also be forgot."

Painted by E. T. Parris. Engraved by C. A. Ferrier.

> Pania   LOOK TO THE PORTALS,
> AND WITH YOUR BEST SPEED TO THE WALLS WITHOUT
> YOUR ARMS! TO ARMS! THE KING'S IN DANGER, MONARCH!
> EXCUSE THIS HASTE,——'TIS FAITH.
>
> SARDANAPALUS

Published by Smith Elder & Co Cornhill London

SARDANAPALUS.

Painted by Parris.] [Engraved by Periam.

THE Sardanapalus of history is luxurious, effeminate and cowardly. His tastes, his occupations, and his habits are those of the slaves who surround him, and with whom all his hours are spent. When, after a protracted siege, all hopes of safety are at an end, without sufficient courage to pass

"One crowded hour of glorious life,"

in wreaking vengeance on the conspirators against his life and crown, he makes a funeral pile of his treasures, his slaves, and of himself.

The poet's hand has garlanded this image with so many fair and delicate flowers, has invested him with so many noble and touching characteristics, that, like the Ionian Myrra, we admire and love, in the midst of doubt and disapprobation. The atmosphere through which we observe him obscures our mental perception. It is laden with perfumes, vocal with song, sparkling with gems, rich in forms of female loveliness, and hallowed by the presence of devoted affection.

"The lute,
The lyre, the timbrel; the lascivious tinklings
Of lulling instruments, the softened voices
Of women ——"

are appropriate accompaniments to their chief, who seems royal still, though with his head discrowned, save by a tiara of gems, and his hand unsceptred, save by the wine-cup. His very voluptuousness takes the form of universal love and benevolence. He wishes to make life

> " One long summer's day of indolence and mirth,"

not to himself only, but to all his subjects. He would not " bruise the flowerets with the armed hoofs of hostile paces," that his people might be crowned with them in their revelry.

Treason and revolt, however, are at work, and their tidings reach him in his illuminated palace, seated amongst his guests; and whilst the portentous elements mingle their warning thunder with the voice of flattery and song. It is then that the reveller blazes out into the hero, and Sardanapalus rushes half armed into the thickest of the fight.

The conception of this character is so beautiful, that we do not stay to inquire whether it be natural. The land of luxury is not the soil that usually produces warriors; but deprive Sardanapalus of his valour, and our respect is extinguished. As the portrait now stands, we worship its beauty, without wishing it to be more like the original.

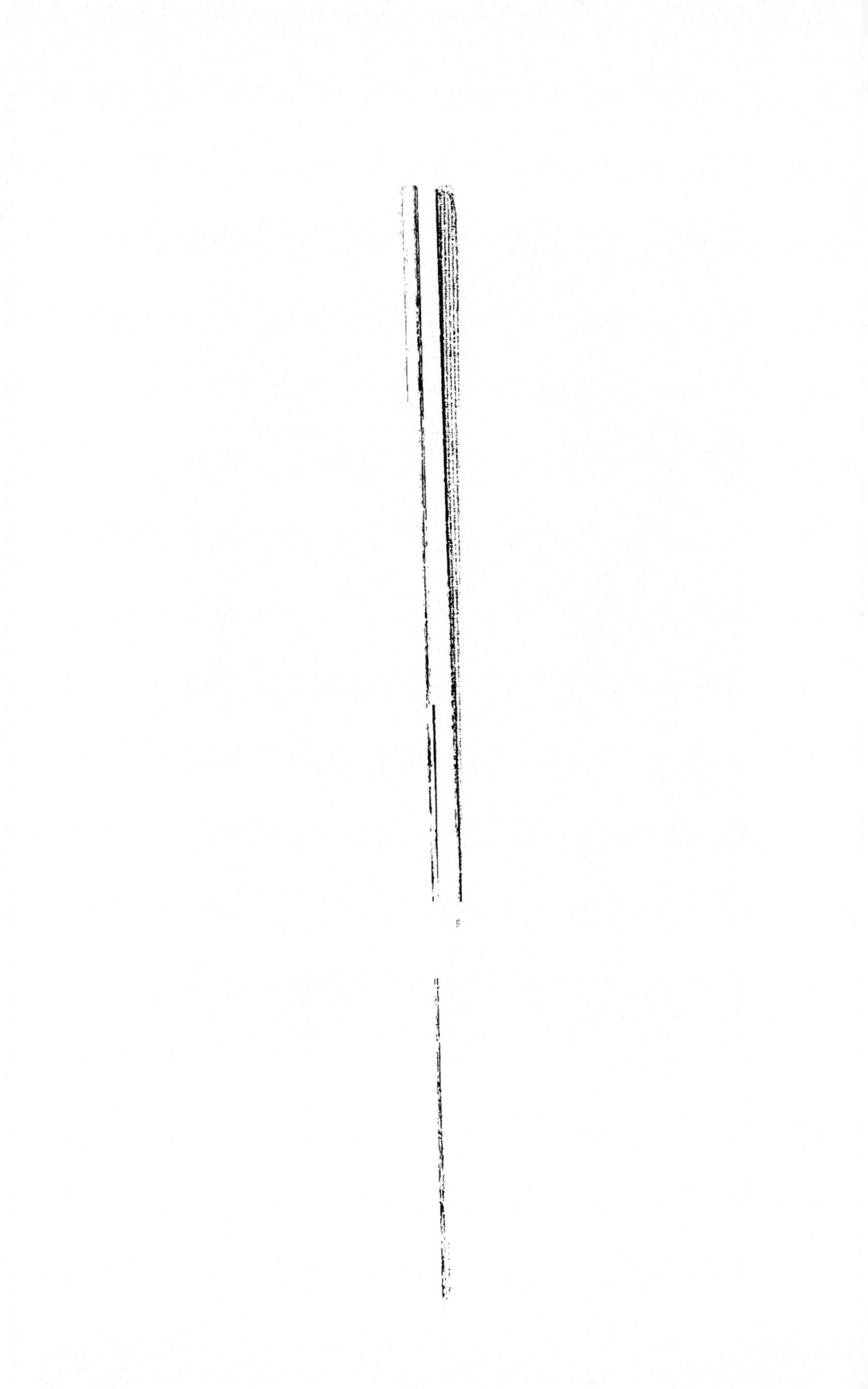

Painted by S. E. James.   Engraved by E. J. Portbury.

Doge.   MY SON, YOU ARE FEEBLE; TAKE THIS HAND.
Jac. Foscari. ALAS! MUST YOUTH SUPPORT ITSELF ON AGE,
             AND I WHO OUGHT TO BE THE PROP OF YOURS?
Loredano.   TOUCH IT NOT, FOSC.; 'TWILL STING YOU. TAKE MINE.
Marina.   SIGNOR, STAND OFF!

THE TWO FOSCARI.

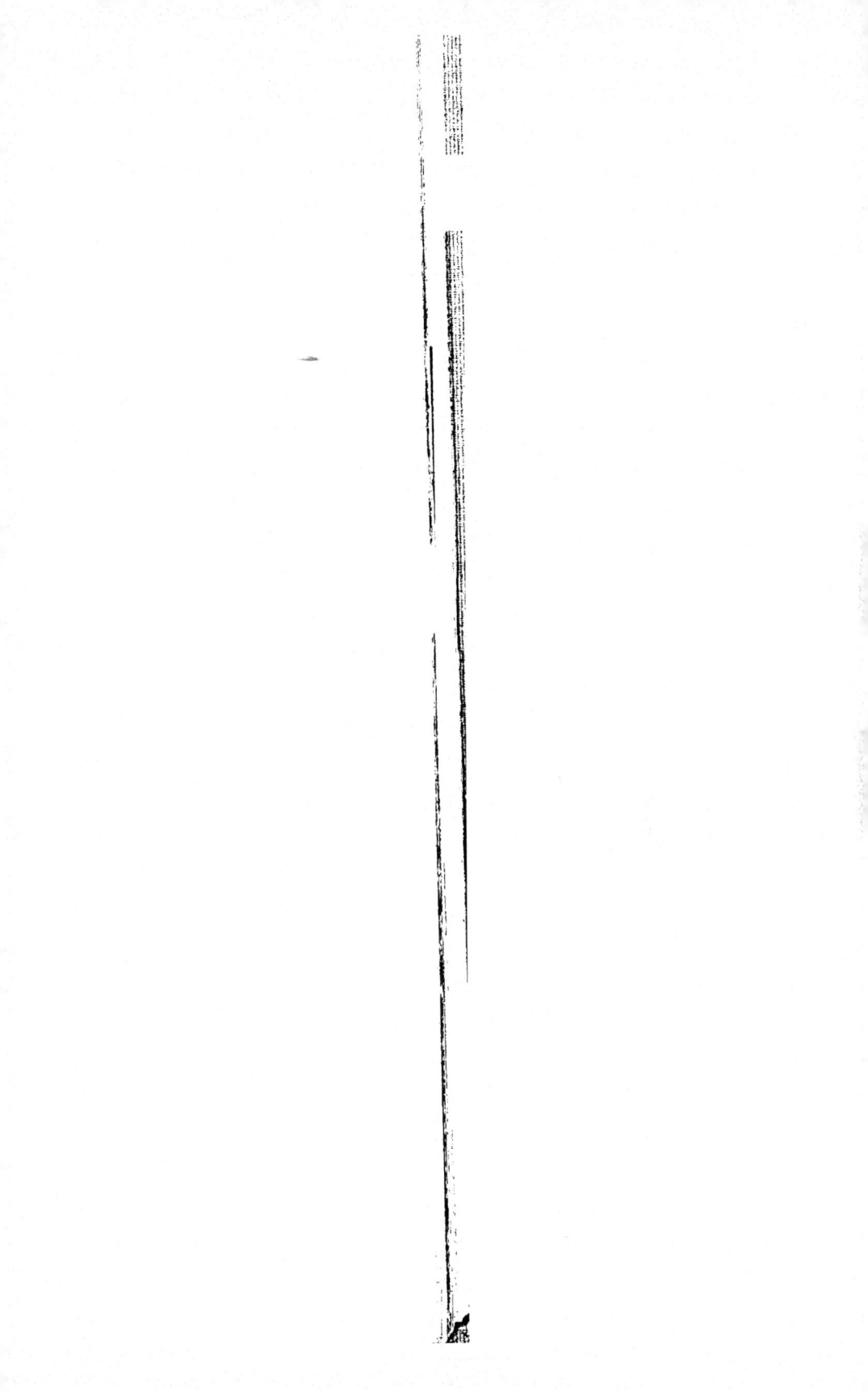

THE TWO FOSCARI.

Painted by Jones.]   [Engraved by Portbury.

In 1445, Giacopo, the only surviving son of Francesco Foscari, was denounced to the *Ten* as having received presents from foreign potentates. The offence, according to the law, was one of the most heinous which a noble could commit. Even if Giacopo were guiltless of infringing this law, it was not easy to establish innocence before a Venetian tribunal. Under the eyes of his own father—compelled to preside at the unnatural examination,—a confession was extorted from the prisoner on the rack; and from the lips of that father, he received the sentence that banished him for life.

Some time after, being suspected, on slight grounds, of having instigated the assassination of a chief of the Ten, the young Foscari was recalled from Treviso, tortured again in his father's presence, and not absolved, even after he resolutely persisted in denial unto the end.

Banished once more from his country which, notwithstanding his wrongs, he still regarded with passionate love; excluded from all communication with his family; torn from the wife of his affections; debarred from the society of his children; and hopeless of again embracing those parents, who had already far outstripped the natural term of human existence, his imagination ever centered on the single desire to return. For this purpose he addressed a letter to the Duke of Milan, imploring his good offices with the senate; and for the heavy crime of soliciting foreign intercession with his native government, Giacopo was once more " raised on the accursed cord no less than thirty times" under the eyes of the unhappy Doge ; and when released, was earned to the apartments of his father, torn, bleeding, senseless and dislocated, but unchanged in purpose. Neither had his enemies relented—they renewed his sentence of exile, and added that its first year should be spent in prison. Such are the historical facts on which Lord Byron has founded his tragedy. The scene chosen by the painter is where Giacopo, supported by his father and his wife, leaves the dungeon to proceed to the place of his banishment.

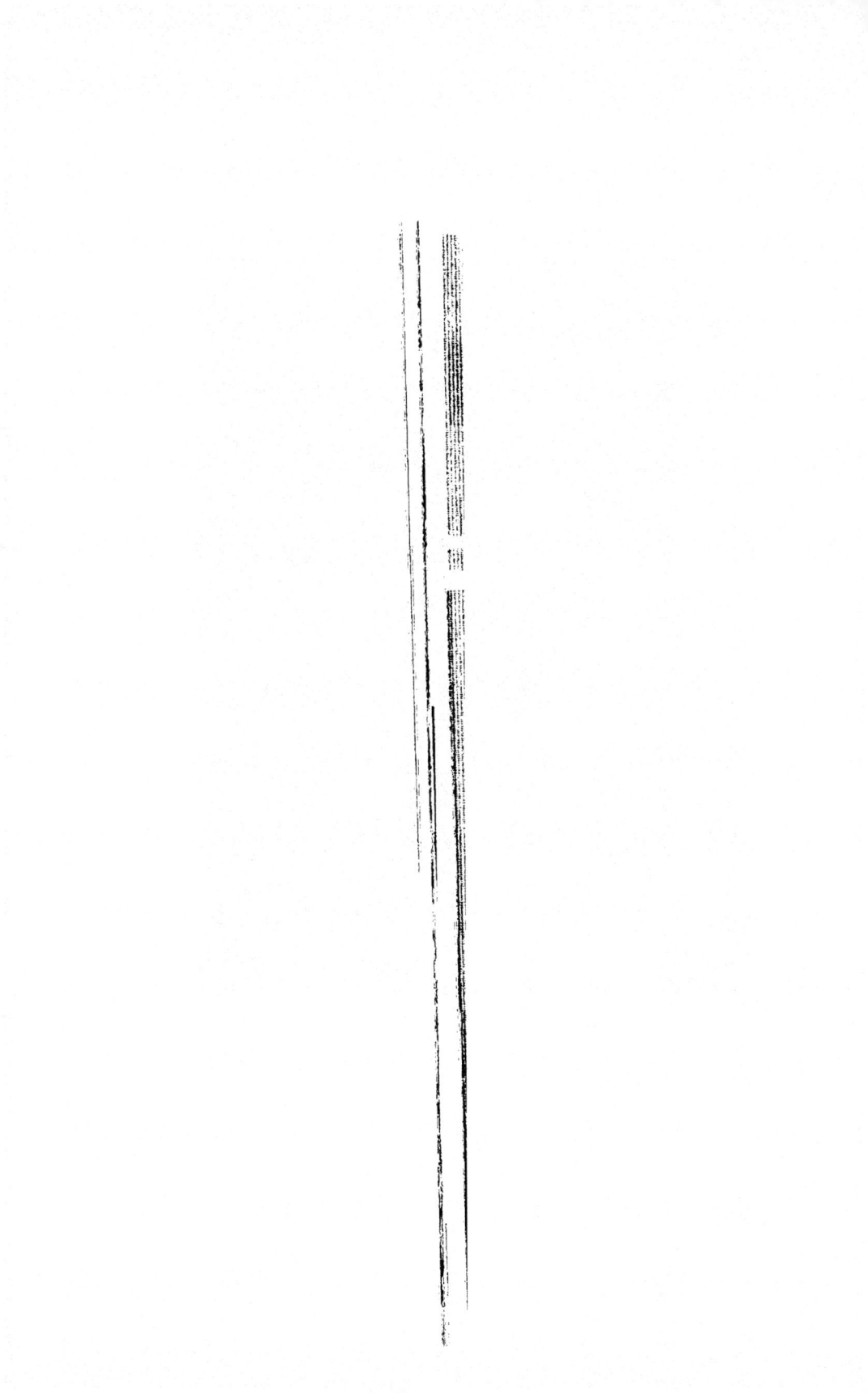

Painted by T. Stothard R.A. Engraved by E. J. Portbury.

Doge I
WILL NOW DESCEND THE STAIRS BY WHICH I MOUNTED
TO SOVEREIGNTY — THE GIANT'S STAIRS, ON WHOSE
BROAD EMINENCE I WAS INVESTED DUKE

THE TWO FOSCARI

Published by Smith, Elder & C° Cornhill, London

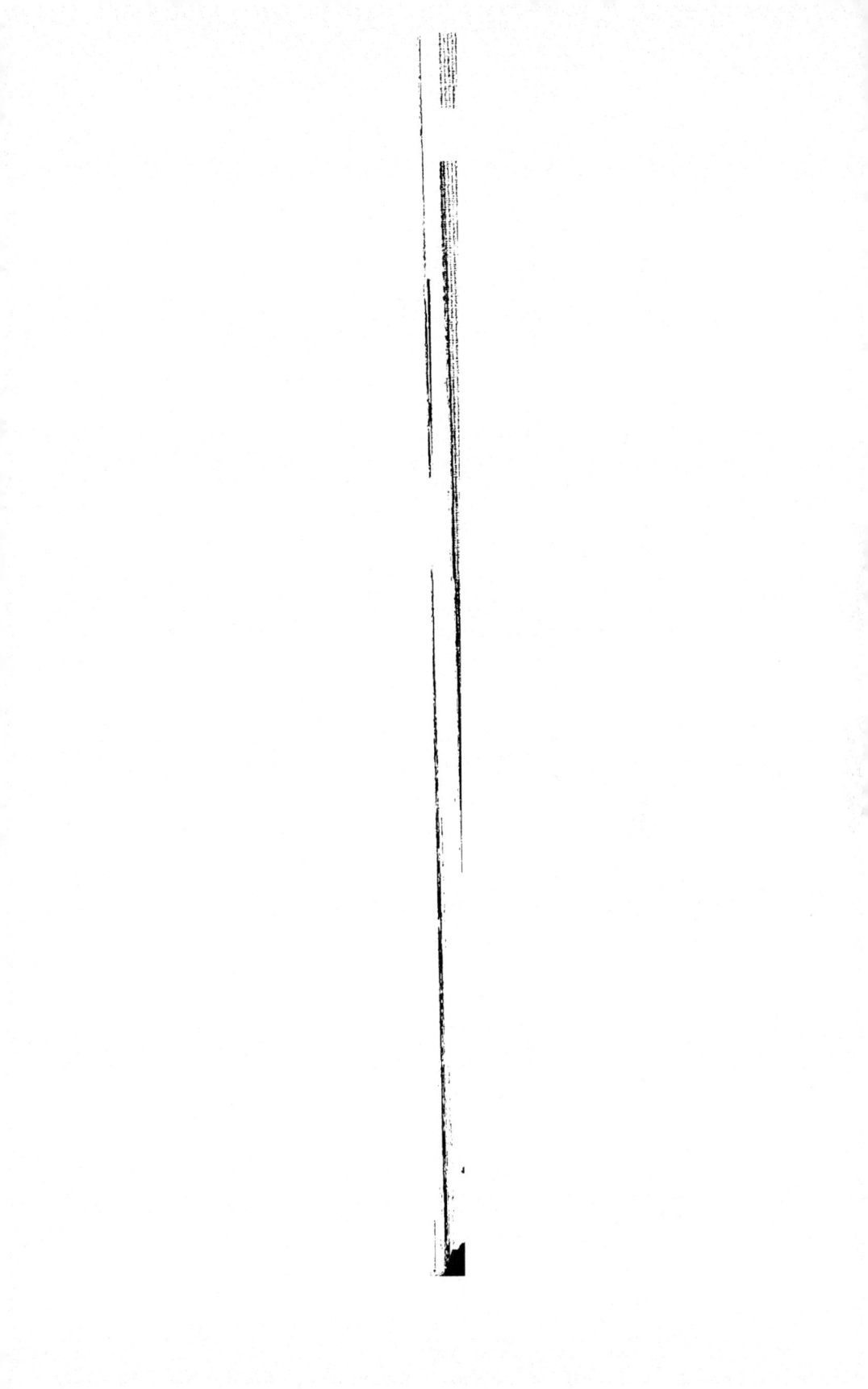

THE TWO FOSCARI.

Painted by T. Stothard, R.A.]   [Engraved by E. J. Portbury.

ARDENT, enterprising, and ambitious of the glory of conquest, it was not without much opposition that Francesco Foscari had obtained his Dogeship; and he soon discovered that the throne, which he had coveted with so much earnestness, was far from being a seat of repose. Accordingly, at the peace of Ferrara, which, in 1433, succeeded a calamitous war, foreseeing the approach of fresh and still greater troubles, and wearied by the factions which ascribed all disasters to the Prince, he tendered his abdication to the Senate, and was refused. A like offer was renewed by him when nine years' further experience of sovereignty had confirmed his former estimate of its cares; and the council, on this second occasion, much more from adherence to existing institutions, than from any attachment to the person of the Doge, accompanied their negative with the exaction of an oath, that he would retain his burthensome dignity for life. In after years, when sorrow for the loss of his four sons, and the extreme feebleness attendant on old age, prevented his attention to the duties of his office, the Council of Ten discharged Foscari from his oath, declared his office vacant, and enjoined him to quit the palace in three days, on pain of confiscation of all his property.

It was suggested that he should leave the palace by a private staircase, and thus avoid the concourse assembled in the courtyard below. With calm dignity he refused the proposition: he would descend, he said, by no other than the self-same steps by which he had mounted thirty years before.

This is the moment embodied by Mr. Stothard in the accompanying illustration.

Drawn by H Pickter．　　　　　　　　　Engraved by H. Cook．

Bertha　　OUT, HUNCHBACK!
Arnold　　　　　I WAS BORN SO, MOTHER!
Bertha　　　　　　　　　OUT
THOU INCUBUS! THOU NIGHTMARE! OF SEVEN SONS
THE SOLE ABORTION!
　Arnold　　　　　WOULD THAT I HAD BEEN SO,
AND NEVER SEEN THE LIGHT!
　　　　　　　　　　　THE DEFORMED TRANSFORMED

Published by Smith, Elder & Co Cornhill, London.

THE DEFORMED TRANSFORMED.

Painted by Richter.] [Engraved by Cook.

ARNOLD, the deformed, stung by the cruel reproaches of his mother, and "weary of his being's heavy load," is about to lay it down, when an evil spirit stops his hand, and promises a remission of his present sufferings, on condition of some future service to be performed. The noblest forms of the heroes of antiquity rise in succession, and he is permitted by the demon to lay down his misshapen body, and to possess the strength and beauty of Achilles.

Next we see him scaling the walls of Rome by the side of the Bourbon, attended by the mocking fiend, (who has animated the form once borne by Arnold,) and spilling blood enough to redeem his infernal pledge. Wading through slaughter and violence, he finds his way to a church, where Olimpia, a beautiful Roman lady, has fled for protection to the high altar. To save herself from the pursuit of the soldiery, she flings a massive golden crucifix on the heads of her assailants, crushing the foremost by its weight; and disdaining offers of safety and protection from Arnold, she throws herself headlong on the marble pavement, from which she is picked up senseless by the hero and his demon attendant; and the act closes.

The last scene represents a wild but smiling country amongst the Apennines, in which, before the gates of a castle, peasants are singing the following chorus.

> " The wars are over,
>   The spring is come;
> The bride and her lover
>   Have sought their home :
> They are happy, we rejoice;
>   Let their hearts have an echo in every voice!"

Were it not given on authority that cannot be doubted, it would seem incredible that the painful dialogue at the commencement of this drama drew its bitterness from the author's experience of maternal cruelty. That a woman, and a mother could regard so trifling a blemish with "the repulsion of actual disgust," and taunt her unfortunate son with a deformity for which, according to some accounts, she was herself answerable, is a circumstance so rare, that it may well be called out of nature. The feminine and maternal impulse would be, like Rudiger in Southey's ballad,

> " To gaze with pity, but to gaze
> With deeper tenderness."

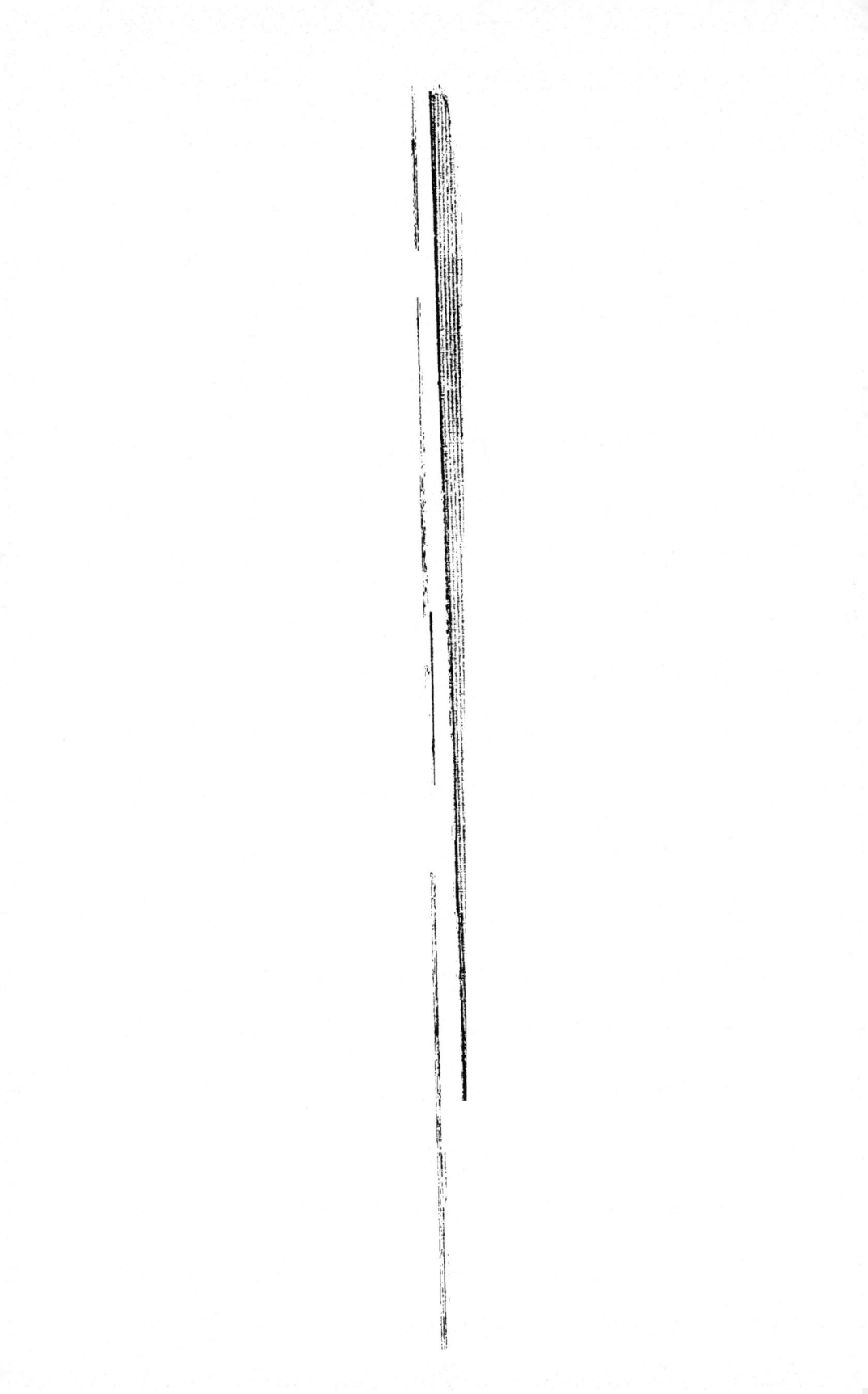

HOURS OF IDLENESS.

Painted by Richter.]   [Engraved by Finden.

" Oh! mark you yon pair; in the sunshine of youth
Love twined round their childhood his flowers as they grew;
They flourish awhile in the season of truth
Till chill'd by the winter of love's last adieu!"

THESE lovely children are intended to represent Lord Byron and one of his juvenile loves. The simplicity and grace of their positions give the idea that the artist must have sketched them by some happy accident, rather than that they had been arranged together for the purpose of composing a picture.

Nothing can be more charming than the slender graceful girl, unless it be the intent look, and natural action of her companion. The luxuriant foliage,—the flowery turf beneath their young feet,—the little birds above them,—the cottage in the distance,—and, above all, the bright and airy effect of the atmosphere, are accessories which admirably accord with the subject:—

" A boy and girl come forth to play
On a sunshine holiday!"
                                    MILTON'S L'ALLEGRO.

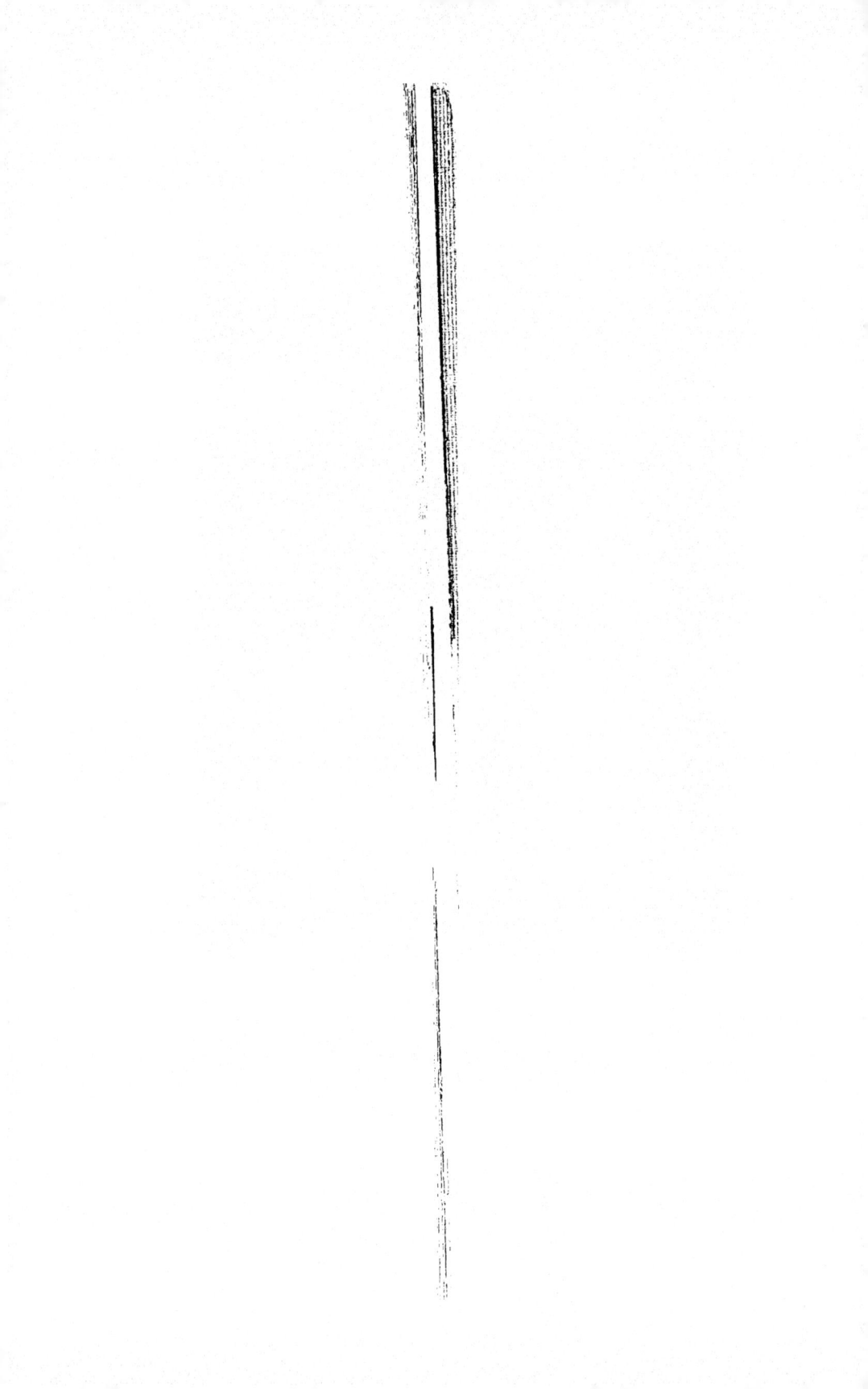

THE WALTZ.

HAIL NIMBLE NYMPH! TO WHOM THE YOUNG HUSSAR,
THE WHISKER'D VOTARY OF WALTZ AND WAR
HIS NIGHT DEVOTES, DESPITE OF SPURS AND BOOTS
A SIGHT UNMATCH'D SINCE ORPHEUS AND HIS BRUTES
HAIL SPIRIT STIRRING WALTZ.

Published by Smith, Elder & Cº Cornhill London

THE WALTZ.

Painted by J. Stephanoff.]   [Engraved by J. Goodyear.

THIS dance, so contrary to the genius of our national character, was introduced from the continent about the year 1811 or 1812, and was forthwith assailed by all the shafts of wit and ridicule, and by all the remonstrances of modesty and good sense. How impotent are any weapons against the dominion of fashion, has been manifest, ever since the beaux of 1100 fastened the points of their shoes to their knees, or Elizabeth legislated against her subjects' ruffs, or Addison inveighed against the monstrous size of the hooped petticoat, which, when elevated to the ceiling, made an awning over the heads of the assembled Club. Shade of Addison! how wouldst thou murmur thy melancholy tones against the lascivious Waltz, and the romping *gallopade!*

Putting aside all question of decency and morality, how ungraceful and unpictorial are these dances! How can a spectator regard with any satisfaction the rushing of the congregated petticoats, or the skirts of the gentleman's coats, standing out with centrifugal force at right angles with their waists? How different from the graceful gliding movement, the steady poise, the swan-like carriage of the head and throat, and the sinking curtsey of the beauties of 1737!

> "Morals and minuets, virtue and her stays,
> And tell-tale powder—all have had their days."

But, say our modern matrons and belles,—" Waltzing is thought nothing of! It is done constantly on the Continent!

nothing but a very prurient imagination can fancy impropriety in an amusement so harmless." We confess ourselves so old-fashioned as to be startled, if, in coming unexpectedly into a lonely chamber, we should find our wife's or daughter's waist thus encircled; and we are sufficiently obtuse to see no great difference between a solitary embrace and one performed in public, except that the latter is the most shameless of the two. The ladies of the present day must be *salamanders*, to live unscathed through such ordeals. "Now a salamander is a kind of heroine in chastity, that treads upon fire, and lives in the midst of flames, without being hurt. She is a perpetual declaimer against jealousy, an admirer of French good-breeding, and a great stickler for freedom in conversation. In short, the salamander lives in an invincible state of simplicity and innocence: her constitution is preserved in a kind of natural frost: she wonders what people mean by temptations, and defies mankind to do their worst."—ADDISON.

We cannot forbear extracting some of the concluding lines of Byron's poem, which sufficiently prove the opinions of one, himself a libertine, whose notions cannot be supposed to have been particularly strict with regard to female propriety.

> " But ye—who never felt a single thought
> For what our morals are to be, or ought;
> Who wisely wish the charms you view to reap,
> Say—would you make those beauties quite so cheap?"
>
> *   *   *
>
> " At once love's most endearing thought resign,
> To press the hand so press'd by none but thine;
> To gaze upon that eye which never met
> Another's ardent look without regret;
> Approach the lip, which all, without restraint,
> Come near enough—if not to touch—to taint:
> If such thou lovest, love her then no more,
> Or give—like her—caresses to a score;
> Her mind with these is gone, and with it go
> The little left behind it to bestow."

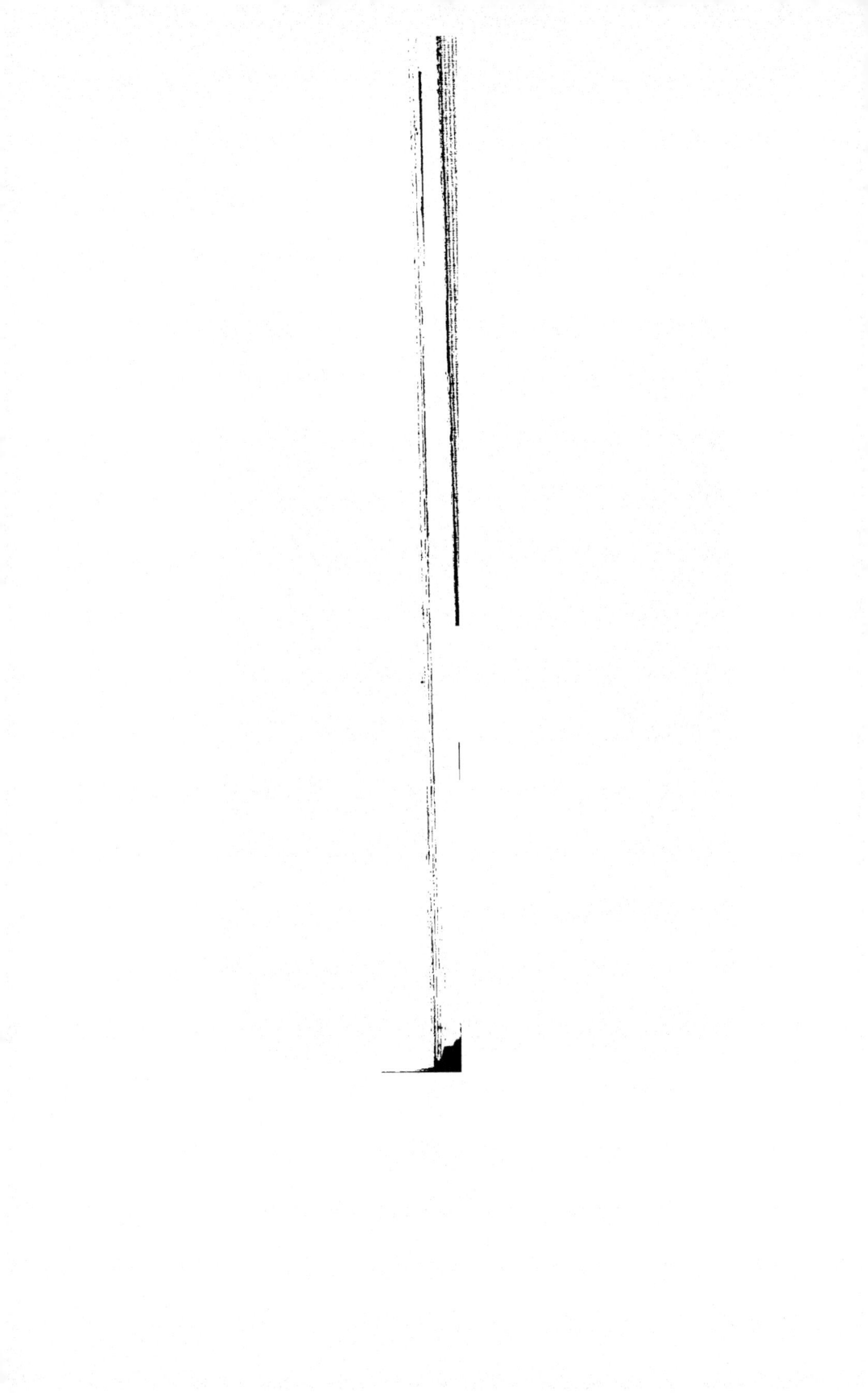

SHE WALKS IN BEAUTY.

ONE SHADE THE MORE, ONE RAY THE LESS,
    HAD HALF IMPAIR'D THE NAMELESS GRACE
WHICH WAVES IN EVERY RAVEN TRESS
    OR SOFTLY LIGHTENS O'ER HER FACE,
WHERE THOUGHTS SERENELY SWEET EXPRESS
    HOW PURE HOW DEAR, THEIR DWELLING PLACE.

HEBREW MELODIES.

Published by Smith Elder & C° Cornhill London.

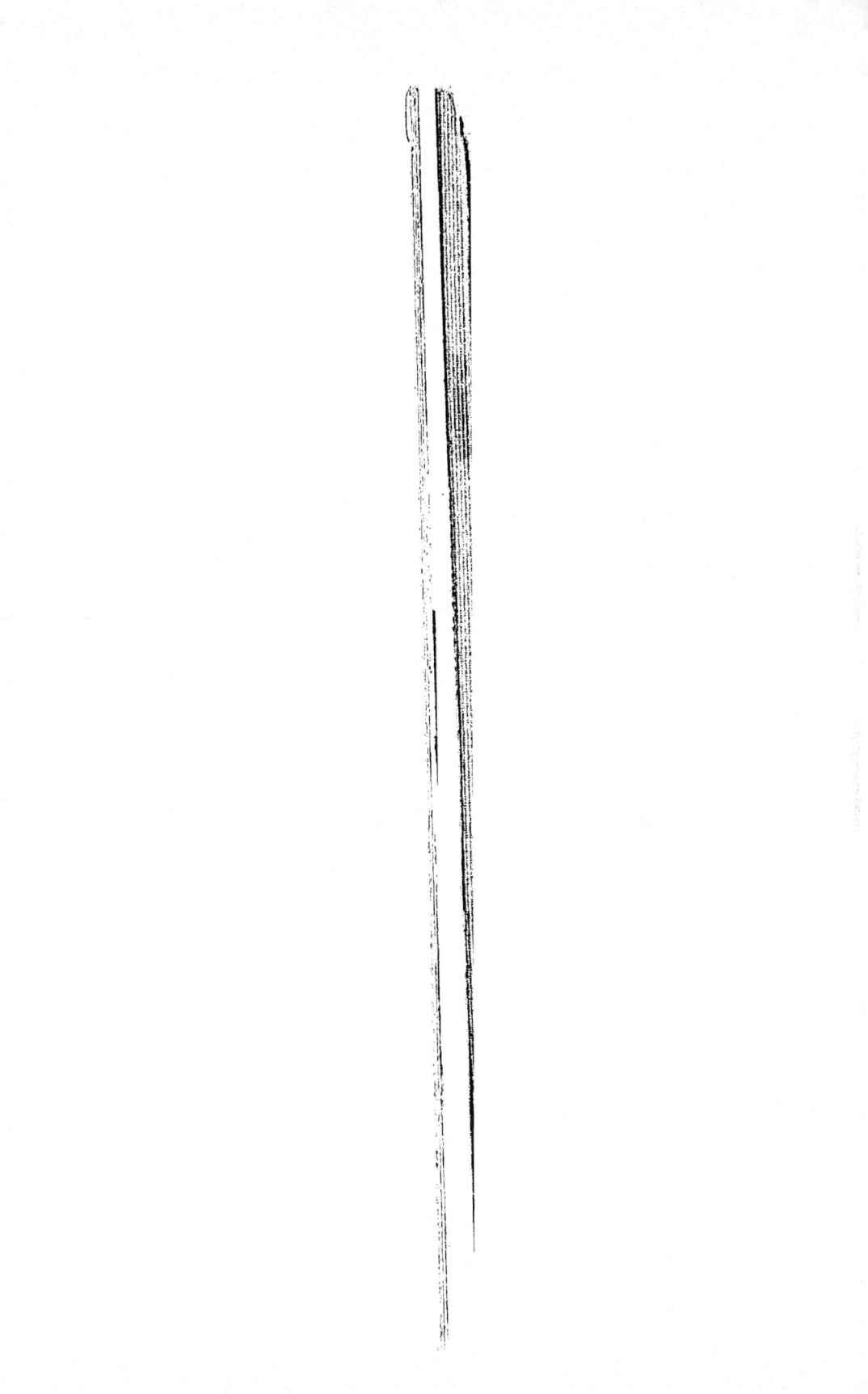

"SHE WALKS IN BEAUTY."

Painted by Richter.]　　　　　　　　　　　　　　[Engraved by Finden.

It is impossible for the power of poetry to conjure up a more beautiful image than that presented to the imagination in the stanzas of which these lines are the commencement. They were written by Lord Byron, one night, on his return home from a ball given by the Duke of Devonshire, where he had seen Mrs. Wilmot, now Lady Wilmot Horton, the wife of his relative, dressed in black crape and bugles; and were presented to her husband on the following morning.

They contain

"Thoughts that not burn, but shine,
Pure, calm and sweet."—MOORE.

And they prove *that* poetry to be most exquisite, which springs, free from the stimulus of passion, and without the taint of sensual feeling.

Pretty as is Richter's personification of this subject, we confess we never look at it, without feeling disappointed by the white drapery, and accompanying angels, that remind us of the absence of resemblance to the object which inspired the poet; nor without longing to see a real, *bonâ fide* portrait[*] of Lady

---

[*] Two, luckily, exist for the satisfaction of posterity; one, a miniature by Mrs. Mee, the other a delightful sketch in oils, by Harlowe.

SHE WALKS IN BEAUTY.

Wilmot Horton, in the dress which she wore on that occasion. But let us be thankful for what we have; for,

> " If Bridgewater to sit there's no compelling,
> 'Tis from her handmaid we must make a Helen."—POPE.

> " She walks in beauty, like the night
> Of cloudless climes and starry skies;
> And all that's best of dark and bright
> Meet in her aspect and her eyes.
> Thus mellow'd to that tender light
> Which heaven to gaudy day denies."

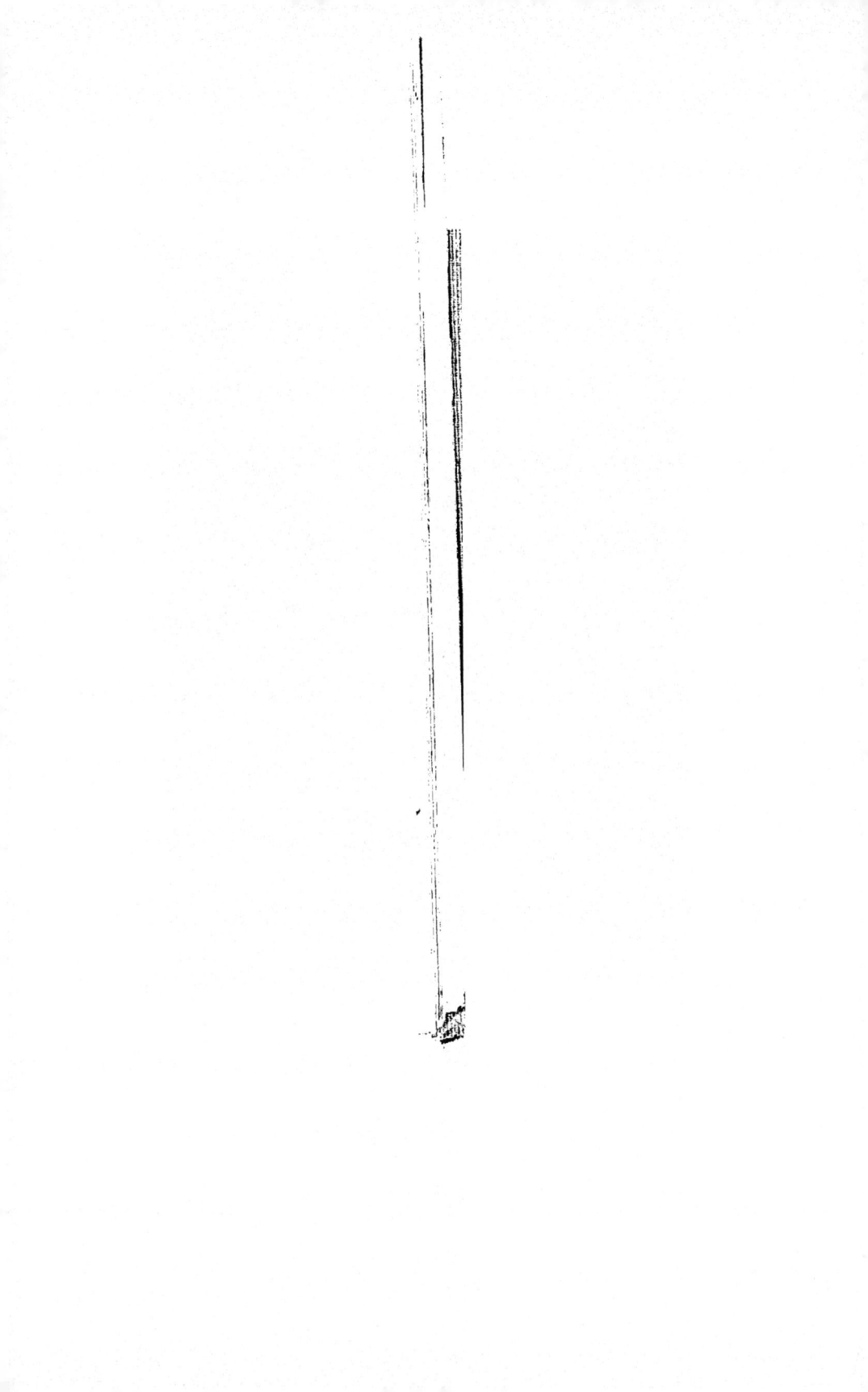

JEPHTHA'S DAUGHTER.

—— THE VOICE OF MY MOURNING IS O'ER,
AND THE MOUNTAINS BEHOLD ME NO MORE
IF THE HAND THAT I LOVE LAY ME LOW,
THERE CANNOT BE PAIN IN THE BLOW!

HEBREW MELODIES.

JEPHTHAH'S DAUGHTER.

Painted by Richter.] [Engraved by Shenton.

HAVING been acknowledged prince of Israel, in an assembly of the people, Jephthah marched against the king of the Ammonites, vowing to the Lord, that if he were successful, he would offer up as a burnt offering whatsoever should first come out of his house to meet him. He vanquished the Ammonites, and ravaged their land; but, as he returned to his house, his only daughter came out to meet him, with timbrels and dances, and thereby became the subject of his vow.

There is something so revolting to our feelings in this apposition of joy and woe—of the gloom of the cypress, with the glitter of the laurel—of the clashing cymbals and songs of triumph, with the tears and lamentations of the innocent victim, that the mind takes refuge in incredulity, and we feel disposed to adopt the opinion of some tender-hearted commentators, who insist, that to live and die unmarried was the extent of the penalty imposed upon her. Jephthah could not have been ignorant that the sacrifice of human victims was odious to God; and, supposing he had devoted his daughter, that he might have redeemed her for a moderate sum of money.

The whole question depends on the acceptance of a single *particle* taken for either *and* or *or ;* for, in Hebrew, the same particle (ו) may signify either. The text may, therefore, without violence be rendered, " Whatever comes to meet me I will devote to the Lord—*or*—I will offer Him up a burnt sacrifice."

JEPHTHAH'S DAUGHTER.

The Fathers, and other learned commentators have, notwithstanding, found no difficulty in acknowledging that Jephthah did really offer his daughter for a burnt sacrifice; and Josephus (Antiq. lib. v. cap. 9.) expressly says, that he did so. This opinion has been adopted by Lord Byron in the following poem, which he has made the vehicle of such noble and affecting sentiments.

I.

"Since our country, our God—oh, my sire!
   Demand that thy daughter expire;
Since thy triumph was bought by thy vow—
   Strike the bosom that's bared to thee now!"
   *   *   *   *   *

V.

"When this blood of thy giving hath gush'd,
When the voice that thou lovest is hush'd,
   Let my memory still be thy pride,
   And forget not I smiled when I died."

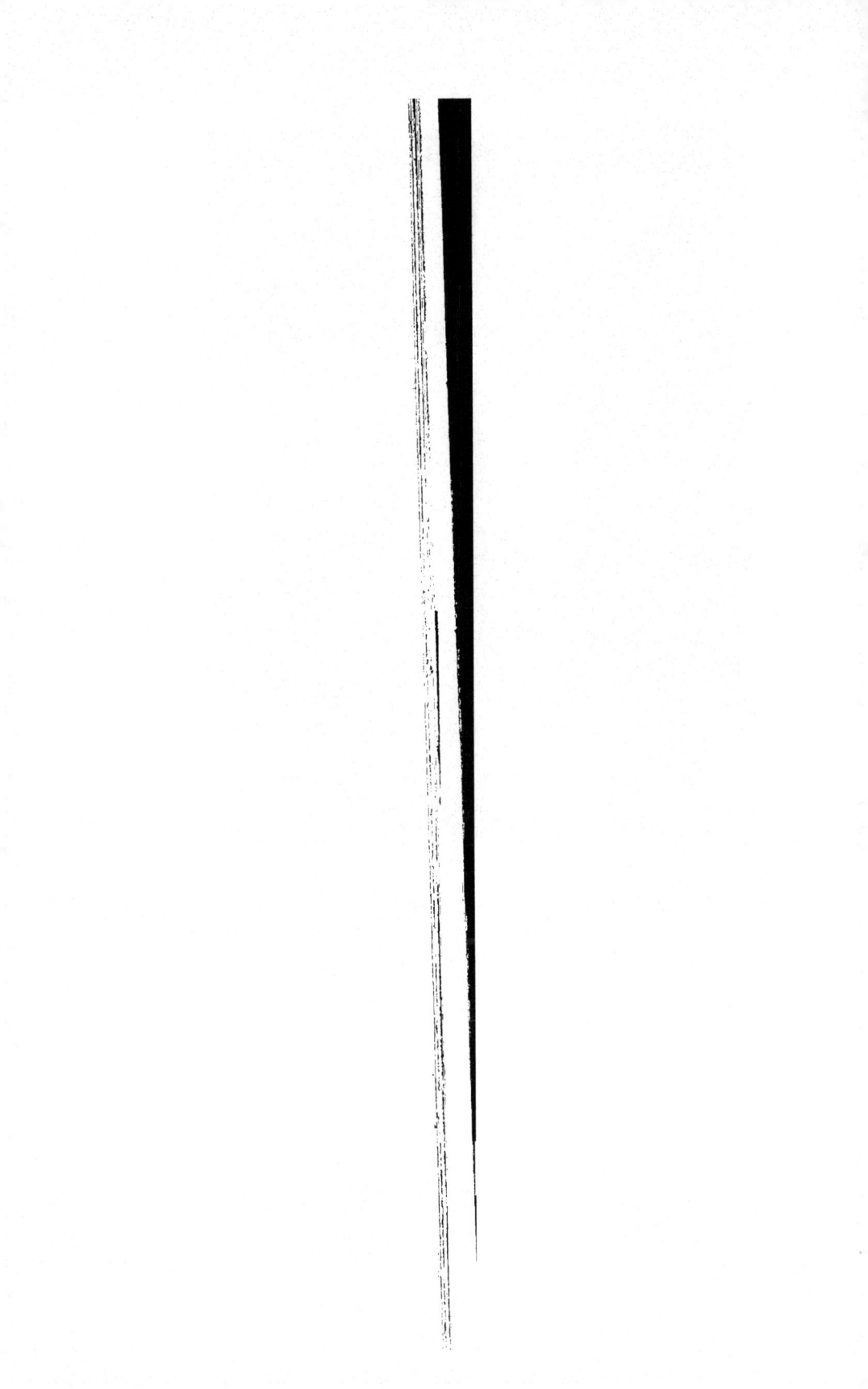

Drawn by H. Corbould. Engraved by J. Goodyear.

THESE TWO, A MAIDEN AND A YOUTH, WERE THERE
GAZING—THE ONE ON ALL THAT WAS BENEATH
FAIR AS HERSELF—BUT THE BOY GAZED ON HER;
AND BOTH WERE YOUNG, AND ONE WAS BEAUTIFUL
THE DREAM

Published by Smith, Elder & Cº Cornhill London

THE DREAM.

Painted by H. Corbould.] [Engraved by Goodyear.

The following extract from Lord Byron's beautiful poem, "The Dream," will best explain the accompanying subject.

> " I saw two beings in the hues of youth
> Standing upon a hill, a gentle hill,
> Green, and of mild declivity, the last
> As 'twere the cape of a long ridge of such,
> Save that there was no sea to lave its base,
> But a most living landscape, and the wave
> Of woods and cornfields, and the abodes of men
> Scattered at intervals, and wreathing smoke
> Arising from such rustic roofs:—the hill
> Was crown'd with a peculiar diadem
> Of trees in circular array; so fixed,
> Not by the sport of nature, but of man:
> These two, a maiden and a youth were there
> Gazing—the one on all that was beneath
> Fair as herself—but the boy gazed on her;
> And both were young, and one was beautiful:
> And both were young—yet not alike in youth.
> As the sweet morn on the horizon's verge,
> The maid was on the eve of womanhood;
> *   *   *   *   *   *
> And on the summit of that hill she stood
> Looking afar if yet her lover's steed
> Kept pace with her expectancy, and flew."

" The old hall of Annesley," says Mr. Moore, " under the name of the ' antique oratory ' will long call up to fancy the

THE DREAM.

'maiden and the youth' who once stood in it; while the image of ' the lover's steed,' though suggested by the unromantic race-ground of Nottingham, will not the less conduce to the general charm of the scene, and share a portion of that light which only genius could shed over it."

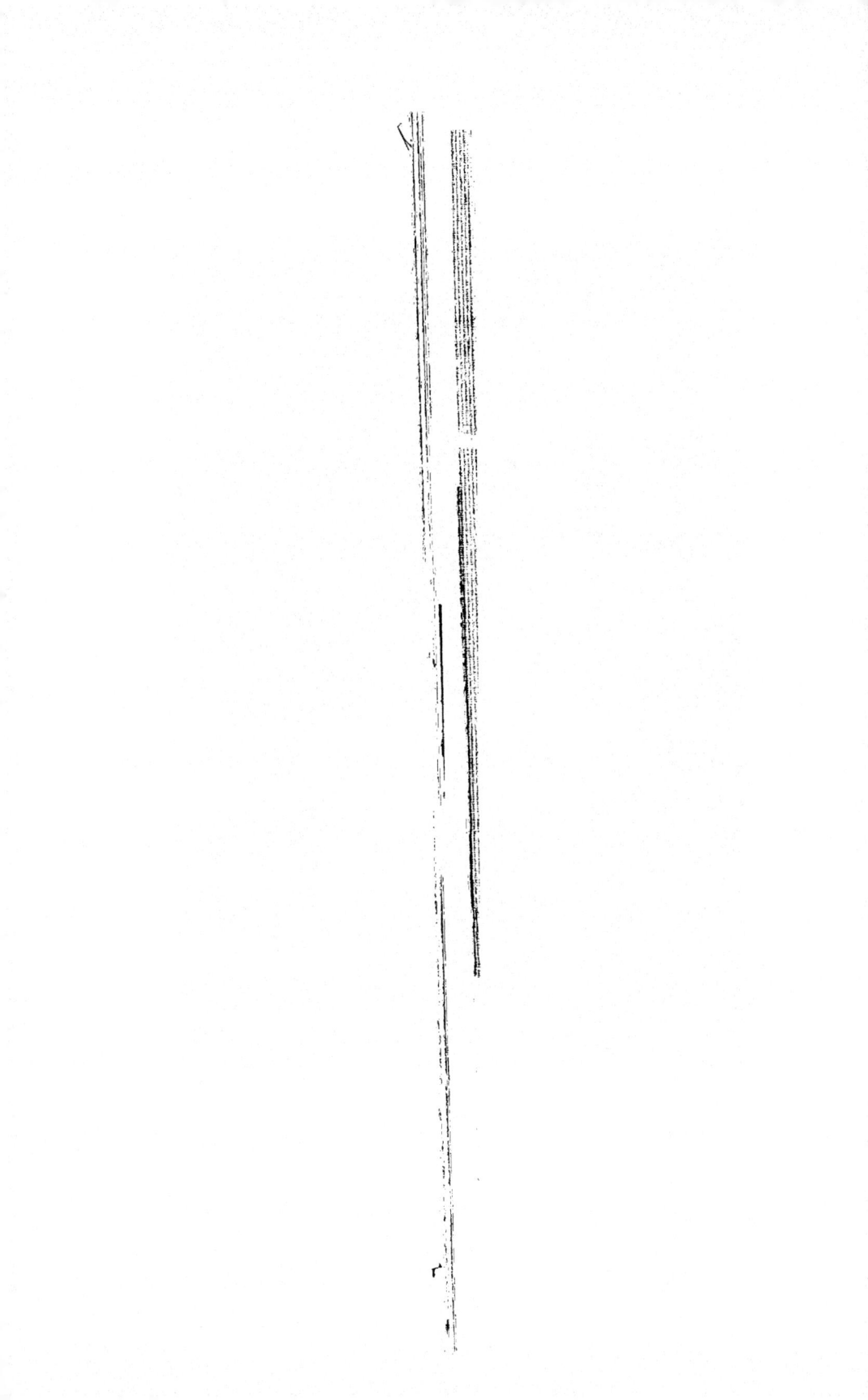

THE MAID OF ATHENS.

THE MAID OF ATHENS.

Painted by Chalon.] [Engraved by Ryall.

A PORTRAIT painter is a sad leveller. He can soften the rugged outline, and sweeten the harsh expression, yet retain the likeness: he may avoid representing an obliquity of vision by a downcast look, or a profile view: he may cover the pertness of a *nez retroussé* by a full-face position of the head: he may purify the sallow complexion till it become clear brown, or tint the sickly white with the rose hues of health.—All this he may do, and yet retain the likeness. But, alas! when the artist has to represent a really beautiful object, how far short will be the "counterfeit presentment" of the lovely original! What pencil can convey the expression, ever changing, ever attractive, and rendered more attractive by movement and change? What combinations of blue, red, and yellow, can imitate the really faultless complexion? It is for this reason that we are generally dissatisfied with, and disappointed in, the portraits of distinguished beauties. Who doubts the loveliness of the Scottish Mary; and yet who has ever seen any single portrait of her, which equalled his notion of the original?

"The art which baffles time's tyrannic claim
To quench it"

is not, however, to be despised, though it only should give us an idea of the manner in which celebrated persons looked and dressed. We can fancy some lovely creature, in 2037, turning over these leaves, and saying or thinking, "was this really the object of Lord Byron's admiration,—the inspirer of his Muse,—the occasion of those beautiful lines,—'Maid of Athens,'" &c.?

THE MAID OF ATHENS.

The accompanying portrait was sketched from Theresa Macri, and was considered to be a good likeness. We say, *was* considered; for, alas! the subject of the picture is no longer young; and it is difficult to think, we have been told by one who has recently seen her, that she ever could have been fair. She was, however, virtuous in youth, and is now, in her riper years, exemplary in the fulfilment of her conjugal and maternal duties.

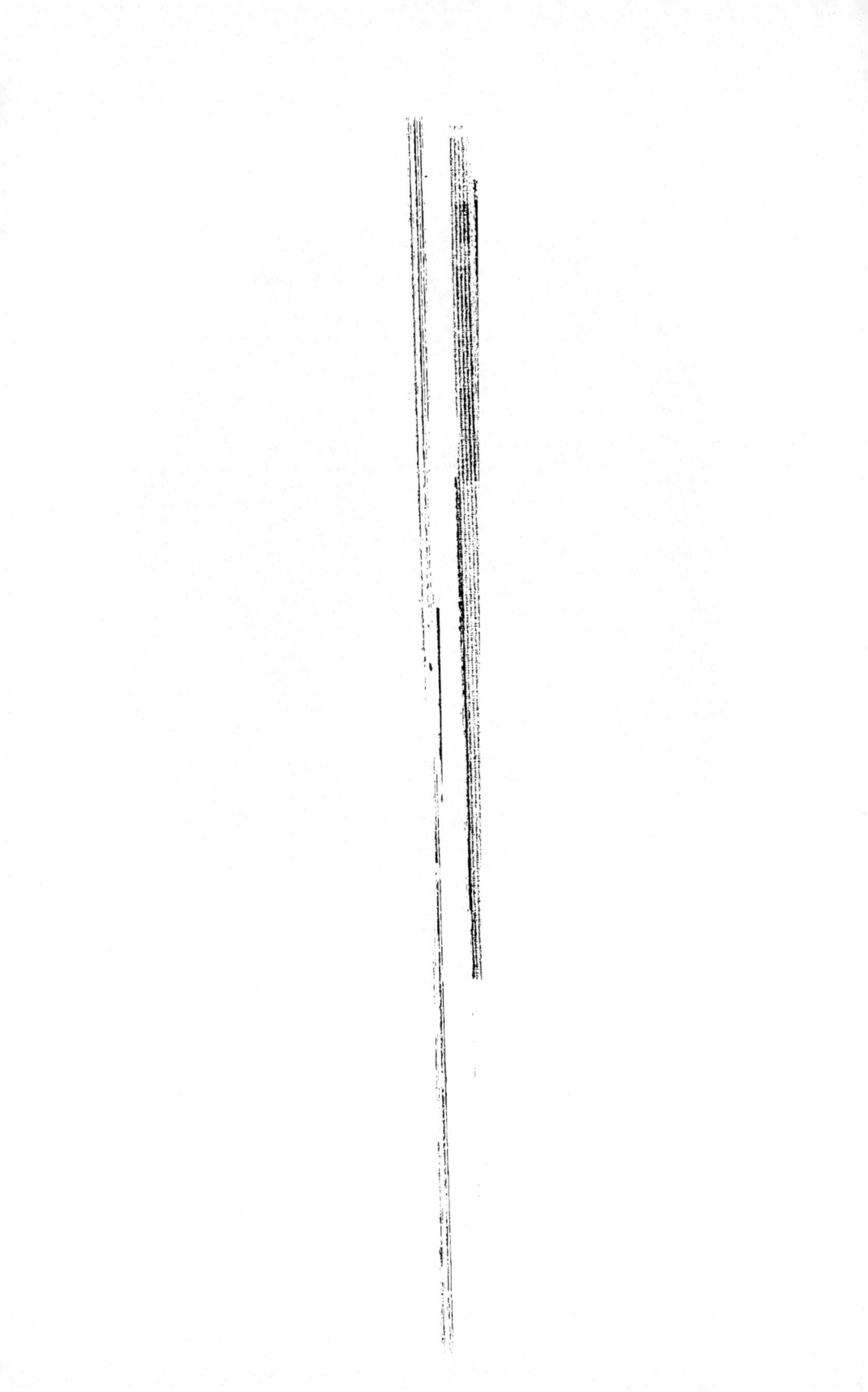

THE COUNTESS GUICCIOLI.

PAINTED BY E. C. WOOD AFTER AN ORIGINAL MINIATURE

Engraved by T. A. Dean

Published by Smith, Elder & Co. Cornhill, London.

THE COUNTESS GUICCIOLI.

Painted by E. C. Wood.]   [Engraved by Dean.

"THE world," says an acute writer of the present day, "is very lenient to the mistresses of poets;" and, perhaps, not without justice, for their attachments have something of excuse, not only in their object, but their origin, and arise from imagination, not depravity. If ever such an attachment could be furnished with an excuse, it must exist in the case of Lord Byron and the Countess Guiccioli, where no domestic affection was severed on his lordship's side, and where, on the part of the lady, the lax morality of the South had rendered a favoured lover no disgrace to a married woman.

Young, noble, handsome and ardent, and with the halo of genius round his brow,—in a climate sacred to poetry, where that genius would receive its full amount of homage,—where is the woman's heart that could have resisted this "group of bright ideas," this galaxy of attraction? Let our countrywomen consider this ere they judge too severely the fair subject of the accompanying engraving. Let them consider also, that no wound was inflicted, either on the affection, or the honour of a husband, who continued to seek the society of Lord Byron, even when he was aware of his attachment to his wife, and who was willing to leave the lovers in tranquillity, provided the sum of 1000*l*., then in the hands of Lord Byron's banker at Ravenna, were paid into his own.

This engraved likeness was taken from a miniature, painted from the Countess at the age of eighteen, and which, at that period was considered extremely like. Some alteration in the disposition of the drapery was necessary to suit the taste of the English public, but the likeness has been carefully preserved.

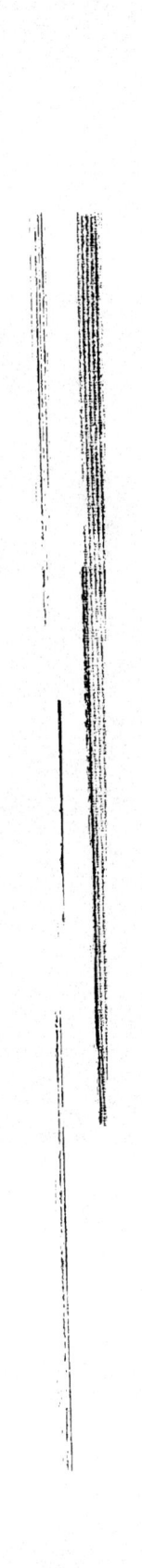

Drawn by H. Richter. Engraved by C. Rolls.

HE THOUGHT ABOUT HIMSELF AND THE WHOLE EARTH
 OF MAN THE WONDERFUL, AND OF THE STARS
AND HOW THE DEUCE THEY EVER COULD HAVE BIRTH,
 AND THEN HE THOUGHT OF EARTHQUAKES, AND OF WARS,
HOW MANY MILES THE MOON MIGHT HAVE IN GIRTH,
 OF AIR-BALLOONS, AND OF THE MANY BARS
TO PERFECT KNOWLEDGE OF THE BOUNDLESS SKIES
AND THEN HE THOUGHT OF DONNA JULIA'S EYES
DON JUAN

Published by Smith Elder & Co Cornhill London.

DON JUAN.

Painted by Richter.] [Engraved by Rolls.

In the mean time Don Juan is not tranquil:

> " Young Juan wander'd by the glassy brooks,
> Thinking unutterable things; he threw
> Himself at length within the leafy nooks,
> Where the wild branch of the cork forest grew."

Sometimes he turned to look upon the rustling leaves of his book; but, to whatever subject of meditation he directed his thoughts, the remembrance of Donna Julia's eyes distracted his attention, and disturbed his philosophy.

> " He pored upon the leaves and on the flowers,
> And heard a voice in all the winds; and then
> He thought of wood-nymphs and immortal bowers,
> And how the goddesses came down to men."

Had he, sagely observes the poet, been well flogged through the third or fourth *form* of a public school, his daily tasks had given him sufficient occupation to have prevented such dangerous reveries. 'Tis droll to see his lordship and good Dr. Watts hit on the same opinion:

> " For Satan finds some mischief still
> For idle hands to do."

" The progress of this passion is traced with consummate knowledge of the human heart; and, but for the seductive colouring with which every incident is embellished, and the air of levity and perfect contempt of all consequences, with which the delusions of passion and the approaches of crime are treated, it might be put into the hands of youth as a moral warning, to guard against the first approaches of irregular desires, and that ophistry of sentiment, by which our impurest wishes and designs are frequently veiled and disguised even from ourselves, till the moment when their gratification seems within our reach. It is then that the mask falls off, and the sophistry, which had seduced, acquires the new duty of apologising for, and excusing, what an unsophisticated view of our own hearts ought to have prevented."

On the discovery of their attachment, Juan is sent on his travels, and Julia expiates her crime in a convent.

Painted by E. T. Parris. Engraved by S S Smith

THOSE LONELY WALKS AND LENGTHENING REVERIES
  COULD NOT ESCAPE THE GENTLE JULIA'S EYES
SHE SAW THAT JUAN WAS NOT AT HIS EASE;
  BUT THAT WHICH CHIEFLY MAY, AND MUST SURPRISE
IS, THAT THE DONNA INEZ DID NOT TEASE
  HER ONLY SON WITH QUESTION OR SURMISE;
WHETHER IT WAS SHE DID NOT SEE OR WOULD NOT
OR LIKE ALL VERY CLEVER PEOPLE COULD NOT.

DON JUAN

Published by Smith Elder & C° Cornhill London.

DON JUAN AND JULIA.

Painted by Parris] [Engraved by Smith.

Don Juan, having lost his father in childhood, is educated by his mother—a lady very learned, and rather hypocritical. Her particular friend is a beautiful young woman, whose fondness for Juan as a child, becomes somewhat less unexceptionable as years roll on, and first youth, and then manhood stamps itself on his brow. The fair Julia first becomes aware of the nature of her feelings, and resolves to make every effort for their suppression.

> " And if she met him, though she smiled no more,
>   She look'd a sadness sweeter than her smile,
>   As if her heart had deeper thoughts in store
>   She must not own, but cherished more the while
>   For that compression in its burning core."

She now resolves never to see Juan again, but finds occasion next day to call on his mother;

> " And look'd extremely at the opening door,
>   Which, by the virgin's grace, let in another;
>   Grateful she was, and yet a little sore—
>   Again it opens, it can be no other,
>   'Tis surely Juan now—"

What the " lady mother mathematical" could have been about, not to perceive the danger of herself and friend, it is hard to say.

> " Whether it was she did not see, or would not,
>   Or, like all very clever people could not."

DON JUAN AND JULIA.

"In the description of the struggles and workings of Donna Julia's mind, with respect to Don Juan, previous to their first and mutual transgression, the poet displays a most consummate knowledge of all the most subtile and refined self-delusions of the human heart. This is, perhaps, the least objectionable part of the poem; since all who choose to avoid the beginnings of evil,—the *sceleris primordia*—all who know the weakness of reason and the strength of passion, may profit by the catastrophe of this amour."

THEY GAZED UPON THE GLITTERING SEA BELOW
    WHENCE THE BROAD MOON ROSE CIRCLING INTO SIGHT,
THEY HEARD THE WAVE'S SPLASH, AND THE WIND SO LOW,
    AND SAW EACH OTHER'S DARK EYES DARTING LIGHT
INTO EACH OTHER

DON JUAN.

DON JUAN AND HAIDEE.

Painted by Parris.]   [Engraved by Smith.

"TEDIOUS as a twice told tale," is the anticipated objection that checks our pen, when about to call the reader's attention to the subjects of our pictorial illustrations; and having had from our earliest youth the poetry of Lord Byron "familiar to our ear as household words," it would almost seem an impertinence to dwell on that which must be known to the reading world generally. We are relieved, however, from the dread that our task is useless, by the conviction that as

> "Through needle's eye it easier for the camel is
> To pass, than Juan's Cantos into families,"

there are many young and pure eyes to whom the perusal of Byron's poetry, and of Don Juan, in particular, is forbidden; and we trust that, after admiring the lovely creatures on the opposite page, they may turn without a feeling of impatience to the explanation which is given of the subject.

Don Juan, a Spanish youth on his travels, is shipwrecked on one of the islands of the Cyclades, and, after sufferings which are fatal to all but himself, he is found on the sands, exhausted and insensible, by a young Greek girl and her attendant, by whom he is watched, and clothed, and nurtured back to life and health. The progress, and tragical termination of the attachment which springs up between "the beauty of the Cyclades" and the stranger, is described with pathos unattained, perhaps, in any other language, as the scene in which it is represented is unequalled in truth and majesty. There are few who have not felt the beauty of a twilight sea-beach; but Byron alone

DON JUAN AND HAIDEE.

has invested it with such richness of imagery, and such vivid reality, that

> "The silent ocean, and the starlight bay,
>   The twilight glow, which momently grew less,
> The voiceless sands, and dropping caves that lay
>   Around them"

strike us as a scene remembered rather than described.

The inhabitants of this scene are worthy their locality:—

> "They look upon each other; and their eyes
>   Gleam in the moonlight; and her white arm clasps
> Round Juan's head, and his around her lies
>   Half buried in the tresses which it grasps;
>   *   *   *   *
> And thus they form a group that's quite antique,
>   Half naked, loving, natural and Greek."

Their interviews take place in the absence of Haidée's father, a Greek pirate, who is, after an absence more than usually prolonged, reported to be dead; and Juan and Haidée are installed as possessors of his dwelling. He returns, to find his daughter consoled for his loss, and to take summary vengeance on the lovers.

PR   The Byron gallery
4377   A new and enl. ed.,
B87   with descriptive letter-
1844   press

PLEASE DO NOT REMOVE
CARDS OR SLIPS FROM THIS POCKET

UNIVERSITY OF TORONTO LIBRARY